A SINGULAR PLURALISM

The European Schools 1984-1994

A SINGULAR PLURALISM
The European Schools 1984-1994

Desmond Swan

Luxembourg – Bruxelles/Brussels I & II – Mol
Varese – Karlsruhe – Bergen N.H. – München – Culham

First published 1996
by the Institute of Public Administration,
57-61 Lansdowne Road,
Dublin, Ireland.

© Desmond Swan

All rights reserved. No part of this publication may be reproduced or transmitted in any form or by any means, electronic or mechanical, including photocopy, recording or any information storage and retrieval system, without permission in writing from the publisher.

British Library Cataloguing in Publication Data

ISBN 1 872002 97 8

Cover design by Butler Claffey Design, Dun Laoghaire

Typeset by Wendy Commins, The Curragh
Printed by ColourBooks, Dublin

CONTENTS

	Foreword	vii
	Introduction	1
Chapter 1	The European Schools: Concept, Controversy and Comment	6
Chapter 2	Curriculum and Assessment: Eliding Foreignness	36
Chapter 3	The History, Governance and Multinational Accountability of the European Schools	67
Chapter 4	The School Communities of Teachers, Parents and Pupils	87
Chapter 5	The European Schools – Their Achievements, Problems and Wider Significance	119
	Notes and References	127
	School Addresses	134
	Index	135

FOREWORD

The publication of Professor Desmond Swan's book on the European Schools is both welcome and timely. Since the Schools have already over forty years of educational experiment and endeavour behind them, it is most appropriate that their history be recorded and that a study be made of their development, achievements and, indeed, of their shortcomings.

No one is better equipped to do this than Professor Swan, who has a distinguished record in the field of education. He has known the Schools intimately for many years and has twice been commissioned to write reports on them.

The publication of his book coincides with a new growth phase of the European Union and of the European Schools. The recent accession of Austria, Finland and Sweden and the prospect of the arrival of a number of Eastern European countries before the turn of the century present the Schools with a considerable challenge. Revealing a deep understanding of their cultural complexity, Professor Swan poses the question of the future of the schools in their present form and ventures to see them in a wider context as models for future European educational development.

On behalf of the Board of Governors of the Schools, I warmly welcome this book. We take pride in the way it records our achievements and will find it invaluable as we seek to adapt to the educational and social demands of the next millennium.

If the making of the Union is to capture the imagination and engage the energies of Europe's youth, education has a vital role to play. In that sphere, the European Schools have much to offer. It is to be hoped that Professor Swan's book will reach and be read by a wide and influential public.

Jørgen Olsen
Representative of the Board of Governors
of the European Schools

INTRODUCTION

Europe is the past, present and future of all the peoples who inhabit the lands lying between the Arctic and the Mediterranean, the Atlantic and the Urals. Traditionally a bitterly divided and warlike continent, it is now, in the European Union, embarked on a voyage of peace. Central to the success of this enterprise must be education, and at the heart of education for a united Europe lie the European Schools.

This study originated in a Resolution of the European Parliament of 7 July 1983 which called for a 'thorough examination of the European School system, in order to assess the extent to which they have fulfilled their original purpose'. This led to an invitation to the author to evaluate and report on the Schools' effectiveness in achieving their aims. That work was carried out in 1984. In 1989 the then Permanent Representative of the Board of Governors, Mr Jørgen Olsen, indicated that a follow-up study would be welcomed. This second evaluative study, added to the first, yielded the longitudinal research reported on here, with a focus across the decade 1984-94.

Looking in from outside at an unfamiliar school system bears some similarity to observing other people's families: intriguing, but fraught with possible misunderstandings. In each case distinguishing between appearance and reality can be a major hazard, complicated as it is by the 'outsider' status of the observer. This consideration, added to the cultural and linguistic complexity of the Schools, argued the need for a long time-scale and a multi-layered research strategy, so as to comprehend a wide range of concepts, structures and regulations, many of which lie beyond the ken of any single European tradition in education.

The research design and strategy used here relied mainly on data collected as follows:

1. Documentary information, supplied by both the European Community's Directorate General for Personnel and Administration, and by the Central Bureau of the European Schools in Brussels.
2. Personal visits to eight of the nine Schools; several visits to some of them.
3. Written and oral submissions solicited and received from Interparents (the combined parents' associations of all the Schools) and from the individual associations of several of them.
4. Submissions from the Primary and Secondary inspectors, as well as attendance at some of their meetings and discussion with many individual inspectors of different nationalities.
5. Documentation, correspondence and discussions with many individual teachers and groups of teachers throughout the Schools.
6. Discussion with and documentation from individual parents and both current and past pupils.
7. Meetings with Members of the European Parliament and of the European Commission, with representatives of the European Trade Union Confederation (ETUC) and of IMCO, the Staff Committee of the Council, as well as with officials of the Belgian and Irish Ministries of Education.
8. Information supplied by Ministry of Education officials in Belgium, Denmark, France, Holland, England and Wales, Scotland, Germany, Ireland, Luxembourg, Greece, Spain and Portugal, partly in response to requests directed through the Irish office of Eurydice, the network of

Introduction

information on education, maintained by the European Union.
9. Replies to detailed questionnaires sent to 14 selected pupils, teachers, inspectors, parents, School Directors and Assistant Directors, of whom 13 responded.
10. Replies to questionnaires sent to the heads of 24 other international schools in France, Belgium, West Germany and Ireland.
11. Personal attendance and participation in the public hearing of the European Parliament's Committee on Youth, Culture, Education, Information and Sport, on the topic of the European Schools, which took place on 26 and 27 November 1986. Reports on the relevant debates of the European Parliament over the years in question.
12. Discussions with many other individuals connected with the Schools from time to time, over the ten-year period, including representatives of the Community Help Service, Brussels.
13. Observation of many lessons in progress by kind permission of the Directors and teachers in Luxembourg, Culham, Bergen, Mol, Varese and both Brussels Schools.
14. Official information and statistics as well as *Schola Europaea*, the pedagogical bulletin published annually by the Central Bureau.
15. Yearbooks of some individual Schools supplied by their Directors.

Research in education frequently takes the form of a once-off cameo shot, since immediate results are often required. The ten-year time-scale of the work reported here began with a Parliamentary enquiry in 1984 and ended with the new statute of 1994. This decade, besides having a certain coherence in itself, gives it some of the character of a time exposure. It has enabled the researcher to gain a close understanding of both the internal dynamics and the external context of this very unusual network of schools, to identify their strengths and assess points of resistance to change where these have become evident. It is hoped that the present case study may contribute not only to making these Schools better known and understood, but also to placing some knowledge of their experience at the disposal of schools and educationalists everywhere, as they face the challenges of the coming millennium. It is also hoped that this book will, like the European Schools themselves, help to bridge the rather wide gaps of understanding that exist between European countries in their reading about and relating with each other's education systems.

ACKNOWLEDGEMENTS

Clearly this study could have been completed only with the help, goodwill and forbearance of many people. To all of them sincere gratitude is expressed. Particular thanks are due to the Board of Governors, the School Directors, to their Assistant Directors, and to all their colleagues, for the spirit of openness and collegiality which they have shown me in the course of this work. I am indebted to the many parents, pupils and past pupils of the schools who gave freely of their time over the years, in response to my requests.

The encouragement of Mr Albert Van Houtte, the informed insight of Mr Pádraig O'Neill and Mr Seán Hunt, former European Schools inspectors, the interest of Mr Denis Healy of Ireland's Department of Education, the trust of Mr R.S. Burke, former member of the Commission of the European Communities, the advice of Mr P.J. Lalor MEP, and the financial support of Ireland's Department of Education are also gratefully acknowledged.

Mr J. Olsen, Secretary General to the European Schools, and his Assistant, Mr Gilbert Pinck, have been most helpful in supplying documentation and answering queries. I am also grateful for the help of Mr Ian Murphy, Director of the European School in Bergen, and of Mr Michael Ryan, a teacher in the Culham School, in checking factual information. Mr Michael Hart, former Director of two European Schools, also deserves my thanks for help at various stages. Help in translating certain documents was received from Veronique Didon, Jeannie Zomerdyk, Rosangela Barone, Dr Ethna Swan, Jennifer Morgan, and from Sara, Niamh and Clíona Swan; to all of them, my thanks. My gratitude goes to Mrs Alice Byrne for typing the manuscript and to my wife, Mary, for her endless optimism and patience.

Articles by the author dealing with various aspects of the European Schools have been published as follows:

'The European Schools – Tower of Babel or Brave New World?', in *Irish Educational Studies,* Vol.8, No.1 (1989), 160-79.
'The European Schools: A New Concept in Multi-cultural Education', in *Curriculum,* Vol.12, No.3 (1991), 138-42.
'The European Schools – Pioneers of Intercultural Education for Europe', in J. Coolahan (ed.), *Teacher Education in the Nineties: Towards a New Coherence.* Limerick, Mary Immaculate College for Association for Teacher Education in Europe, Vol.1 (1991), 205-20.
'The European Schools: Cultural Fusion or Cultural Fission?', in *Schola Europaea, 1953-1993.* Brussels, The European School, 40 Rue d'Arlon, 83-88, 1993.

(The reader should note that the use of the masculine form of pronouns or adjectives to include the feminine meaning throughout this work is not to be interpreted prejudicially.)

Chapter 1

THE EUROPEAN SCHOOLS: CONCEPT, CONTROVERSY AND COMMENT

Les Écoles Européennes ... une audacieuse initiative.
Paul-Henri Spaak (1962)

INTRODUCTION

The nine European Schools constitute a separate, self-contained school system, now in its fifth decade, which has been established and maintained by the European Union, formerly the European Community, by its predecessors and its Member States. They are a novel, distinctive and challenging type of school, aiming to achieve things hitherto unattempted in the history of education. These Schools are remarkable primarily because of their unique multi-cultural, multilingual and multinational character and structure. In particular, they are implementing a new kind of pluralism in schooling, and pioneering a new educational paradigm, matched to the emerging identity of tomorrow's citizens of Europe.

Since the first one was established in 1953, the European Schools have been distinctive in several other ways. Their governance involves the national Ministers for Education of all the

Member States of the European Union, together with the Commission of the EU, with a watching brief held by the European Parliament; their main clientele, a range of highly mobile expatriate families; their curriculum, in part a synthesis of all those of the same Member States, together with their many different languages and separate cultural traditions.

Yet they have, from the beginning, shared a common mandate: to cultivate and work for the ideal of European unity, based on the equal dignity of each of the cultures within it. Despite the waxing and waning of support for it among various Member States themselves, the Schools have remained steadfast in the pursuit of this ideal – a matter for which they have not always been given full credit by those who fault them on other matters. Although each successive enlargement of the EU over the years has added to the burden borne by the Schools, they are nevertheless fulfilling this large politico-social mandate with considerable success, though, as we shall see, not without some difficulties.

This study, which is based on the decade 1984 to 1994, provides an independent description and appraisal of the system, both as it changes and as its European context itself changes. This chapter describes the system in general. It highlights some of the Schools' more unusual features and policies, while presenting and assessing public comments on them from diverse sources, in view of their unique context, mission and structures.

No doubt such unusual features will explain the interest that has been shown in these Schools by professional educationalists in different parts of the world. This interest focuses particularly on their pioneering work in bilingual education, and in language teaching in general. Besides, since schooling still tends to be the jealously guarded preserve of the nation state and therefore frequently insulated behind national boundaries, the potential contribution of the European Schools to educational convergence among the different European education systems, at the dawning of post-nationalist Europe, deserves also to be highlighted. Its effects are seen not only in the subsequent lives of their pupils, but also in the influence that the 'European' experience of teachers and inspectors alike can exert on the development of their respective systems when they return to them.

Besides the educationalists, many parents throughout Europe will have a keen interest in the Schools, for personal reasons. They will be among the thousands of actual or prospective employees of the EU and its related institutions who are weighing up the decision to accept employment in Brussels or in another of the eight locations of these Schools in Western Europe (see Figure 1), and for whom the educational facilities available to their family will play a key role in their decision. They want to know what a European School is, and what kind of education it can offer their child. It is hoped that this study will answer some of the questions, both of the parents and the professionals, about this fascinating and sometimes controversial system, and help to make more visible a network of schools that are so widely scattered as to be unknown to very many Europeans.

A School System for Europeans

Each of the European Schools offers its pupils the opportunity, not available everywhere, of a continuous education, usually on one campus, in coeducational classes, from kindergarten through primary and secondary, up to university entrance. This continuity, especially for expatriate children, is a considerable boon. Besides, for many parents, the European School offers the only chance to prevent the separation of their children from their country's curriculum, taught in their mother tongue. A third major attraction for some parents is that, since the Schools were specifically established for the children of employees of the EU and its institutions, priority of admission is given to them, and for them tuition is free. Under certain conditions, other children may be admitted and are charged a tuition fee.

The Schools' admissions policy otherwise is an open one. Yet the fact that they are at once accountable to twelve national governments (fifteen as of 1995), and serve predominantly expatriate, migrant populations, adds both to their cultural richness, to the constraints upon their organisation and curriculum,

Figure 1 Location of the European Schools

1. Culham
2. Bergen
3. Mol
4. Luxembourg
5. Bruxelles I
6. Bruxelles II
7. Karlsruhe
8. Munchen
9. Varese

and to the possibility of misunderstanding arising at any level from classroom to Council.

There are now nine European Schools, with a tenth, which will be the third one in Brussels, being planned to open in 1997.

A Singular Pluralism

Legally they comprise a single unified system which, in the decade 1984-94 was the joint responsibility of the Education Ministers of the twelve sovereign countries which comprised the European Union. Culturally they are an amalgam of the many indigenous traditions of these countries, with their nine major languages, which are represented in microcosm within the Schools. Geographically located in six of these countries, from England to Italy as Figure 1 shows, they are staffed by teachers seconded from the twelve EU national systems, and award a single school-leaving certificate, the European Baccalaureate.

The Schools vary considerably in enrolment, ranging from 721 pupils in Mol to 3,401 in the Brussels I School (in 1994), as Table 1.1 shows.

Already it will be seen that they are considerably more complex than other international schools or even 'company schools'. Besides, the European Schools must pursue their curricular aims on the basis of *equality of esteem* among the Member States, and this to a unique extent, among the major European cultural and linguistic groups represented in them.

Table 1.1 School Enrolments (August 1994)

School	Kindergarten	Primary	Secondary	Total
Luxembourg	411	1,226	1,611	3,288
Brussels I	273	1,153	1,975	3,401
Brussels II	150	918	1,424	2,492
Mol	49	216	456	721
Varese	119	494	622	1,235
Karlsruhe	80	475	687	1,242
Bergen	80	323	435	838
Munich	81	371	548	1,000
Culham	97	304	440	841
Total	1,340	5,520	8,198	15,058

Language and the Schools

This equality is established and expressed primarily in the structuring of the Schools into language sections, each of which uses a different major European language as its everyday medium of instruction. Although there are said to be over 100 languages spoken throughout the Member States, even to have separate language sections teaching through nine different languages across these Schools, with between five and nine individual sections in each School, represents in itself a considerable achievement in implementing the multinational principle, notwithstanding the pedagogical, administrative and financial problems which this entails. The language sections (together with their number, indicated in brackets) are as follows: Danish (4), Dutch (9), English (9), French (9), German (9), Greek (3), Italian (9), Portuguese (2) and Spanish (5), making 59 in all at the time of writing. Their location and distribution are shown by the X marks in Table 1.2.

Table 1.2   The European Schools: Distribution of Language Sections 1993*

School	Grk	Ger	Eng	Dan	Fre	It	NL	Spa	Por
Luxembourg	X	X	X	X	X	X	X	X	X
Brussels I	X	X	X	X	X	X	X	X	—
Brussels II	—	X	X	—	X	X	X	—	X
Mol	—	X	X	—	X	X	X	—	—
Varese	—	X	X	X	X	X	X	—	—
Karlsruhe	—	X	X	—	X	X	X	—	—
Bergen	—	X	X	—	X	X	X	X	—
Munich	X	X	X	—	X	X	X	X	—
Culham	—	X	X	X	X	X	X	X	—

*Data supplied by Central Office of the European Schools, August 1994.

The structure of the Schools represented in Table 1.2 means that a pupil from any Member State is taught most subjects through his or her mother tongue, provided the School has such a language section. This section constitutes the pupil's 'home base', providing important linguistic and cultural continuity with his home country.

However, besides being taught mainly through their mother tongue, at least during their primary schooling, each pupil must also study a second language from the first grade primary. The role of this second language as a medium of instruction (*langue véhiculaire*) for other subjects gradually increases with transfer into secondary. Indeed some pupils (e.g. the Belgians and the Irish) will study a third language where this is an obligatory component of their home country's curriculum.

Such features as these, together with harmonised French, English and German curricula and the mandatory 'European ideal', distinguish the European School from the typical international school. In the latter, one, or at most two, cultural orientations will predominate, with the emphasis on *assimilation*, whereas here no one national culture or nationality is dominant, while the emphasis is on *pluralism*. Each national group is a minority, enjoying in principle equal status with the rest as of right and, since they serve pupils both coming from and returning to their separate national systems, these Schools' curricula seek as far as possible to synthesise and dovetail with the school curricula of all twelve – now fifteen – with their individual cultural and historical traditions. This remains true even where a national group (the Belgians, the Luxembourgers, the Austrians and the Irish) will not have a dedicated language section of its own, and effort is needed in such cases to guard against the *de facto* assimilation of these with, say, the French, Germans or British.

This is clearly a very complex arrangement in which the national language or *lingua franca* – sometimes more than one – of each of the twelve States is taught by teachers whose mother tongue it is. School policy, however, dictates that only three of these languages (French, English and German) are used as *langues véhiculaires* or media of teaching certain other subjects as well, and this compromise does confer a greater prominence, with no doubt a certain status, on these languages. While it is quite understandable, this policy could intensify isolation by precluding other learning possibilities, e.g. for non-Dutch children in Bergen and for non-Italian children in Varese.

Against this, however, must be weighed the fact that some of the largest Member States – for example France, Britain and Germany – already have their own network of *Auslandsschulen* or 'schools abroad', which offer their own nationals, at least in Brussels, an alternative, if often expensive, source of education in their mother tongue. But some of the smaller, as well as the more peripheral, Member States provide no such alternative. The European Schools therefore offer parents from these countries a unique, if qualified, opportunity of education for *their* children, taught by teachers from their home country, in the national language and idiom, and without breaking up the family unit. It is an opportunity which many parents value very highly indeed, and is a crucial factor for many of them in considering employment with the EU or a related institution away from home.

Again, Article 5 of the Statute requires that the duration of studies undertaken, the diplomas and certificates awarded, and especially the European Baccalaureate, be fully recognised *throughout the EU* as equivalent to the local school-leaving certificate, for the purpose of admission to universities and similar institutions. Following some initial hesitation (e.g. in some French and British institutions) this procedure is now well established, giving qualified school-leavers immediate access to universities in their homeland and in fifteen other European countries. For many, this will be the greatest attraction of this complicated and extraordinary school system.

Some Public Comment on the European Schools

Such an unusual, innovative and ambitious educational project was bound to attract the attention of Members of the European Parliament, journalists and other public figures, no less than educationalists and prospective European civil servants. As pioneering institutions, they could scarcely avoid controversy.

Ten years after the establishment of the Schools, Jean Monnet, whose own daughter had been a pupil at the Luxembourg School, maintained in 1962 that: 'The success of the European Schools demonstrates that in future Europe can have its culture without the nations which comprise it losing theirs' (Monnet 1962). On the occasion of their fortieth anniversary in 1993, the President of the Commission of the European Communities, Jacques Delors, wrote: 'Les écoles ... sont en effet devenues un laboratoire sociologique et pedagogique *unique au monde*, et irremplaçable pour la création d'une structure scolaire Européenne' (Delors 1993). To the educationalist Vernon Mallinson in 1980, the Schools were 'something quite new in the history of educational institutions', while politically he found in them 'a striking example of committed movement towards the attainment of a unified EEC Community' (Mallinson 1980). Similarly William D. Halls described them in 1974 as 'a (flourishing) witness to the success of a gradualist policy in educational matters' (Halls 1974). Lastly, Michael Hart, who has been headmaster in two of the Schools (Mol and Luxembourg), saw them as 'a bold and imaginative attempt to provide common education ... for the children from all the Member States'. However, he went on to maintain that 'they fail ... to provide complete secondary education for less able pupils' (Hart 1989).

On the other hand, Guy Neave (Neave 1984) saw them as contradicting both the EC's general policy for the education of migrants' children and the principle of equality of educational opportunity. Indeed, Neave was critical of the EC for not having extended this principle to its immigrant population, then numbering 12 million. Perhaps this argument would have more validity if the (then) EC as such *did* in fact have full responsibility for the education of all its immigrants or again if it were ever to be accorded a determining voice in formulating education policy as a whole for the Member States. But neither is the case to date. Education as an area of responsibility for the EC was eschewed in the drafting of the Treaty of Rome and has always been a most sensitive issue when it has been discussed at ministerial level. Legally the EU is not involved in policy-making for, and has no direct role in, education in the Member States, although it has an indirect one, enacted mainly through its Task Force on Human

Resources, Education, Training and Youth and Sport, which has now become Directorate-General (DG) XXII. It has established a number of programmes in specifically targeted aspects of education and training in which these States may choose to become involved if they so wish, thereby paralleling to some extent the role of the United States' Federal Government in the education systems of the States of the Union.

But the European Schools remain a separate matter from DG XXII and its remit, having been founded primarily to serve the needs of the families of employees of the EU and its related institutions. And while the Schools have admitted children not only from the Member States but from dozens of other nations too, they are attended not only by children of professional families, as Neave maintains, but by children of other social groups; for example, many Italian miners' children have attended the School at Bergen. Thus while they, along with the European University Institute in Florence and the College d'Europe at Bruges, constitute unique initiatives of the EU in education, they can scarcely be criticised for failing to undertake responsibilities that belong not to them but to the national education authorities in the Member States.

THE EUROPEAN SCHOOLS AND THE EUROPEAN PARLIAMENT

A wide range of views on the Schools were expressed in the European Parliament in its several debates on the European Schools, including those of 1983 and 1993; indeed it went so far as to block the funding of these schools temporarily in 1992 and again in 1993. This Parliament has 518 members directly elected by the citizens of the fifteen Member States, with all the political, cultural, educational and ideological diversity that this implies. Between 1966 and 1993 there were six reports and four resolutions of the Parliament dealing with various aspects of the Schools (European Parliament 1993), while the Commission cosponsored a conference which considered the Schools in the context of intercultural and European education in 1989 (EEC 1990). Rather than dwell on these in detail, some flavour of the range of views expressed here from time to time may be gleaned from the following selection of quotations from the 1983 debate (European Parliament 1983).

Dealing specifically with Mr Papapietro's report to the Parliament on the European Schools in 1983, the rapporteur himself described them as 'a genuine laboratory for the formation of European and Community pedagogy, cultural interaction and ethical and civil environment'.

Mrs J. Buchan, a Socialist member, described the Schools as being 'more elitist than we would tolerate in the state school systems'. Mr Pedini (European People's Party) felt they were worth promoting 'so as to be able to use the experience gained there as a means of Europeanising the attitudes of the national schools'. Describing them as 'a unique system of education', Mr E. Kellett-Bowman (European Democrat) expressed a common British view when he saw them as being 'basically founded upon the French system with some ideas incorporated from other systems'. The 'elitist' charge was reiterated by Mr Alvanos (Communist), while Ms Pruvot felt that the 'unique opportunity' afforded by this 'unparalleled system of European education' was being hindered by legal, administrative, organisational and financial problems. Mrs Pery, another Socialist member, criticised the Schools for creating 'educational failures'. Mr Bogh (Christian Democrat), while conceding that such Schools faced immense educational problems, wondered why a mundane function like everyday education must be turned into 'a messianic mission for European union'. In short, while some praised the Schools, the general tenor of this debate was more negative than positive towards them.

Further public comments are found in the unpublished evidence presented on 26 and 27 November 1986 to a special hearing of the European Parliament's Committee on Youth, Culture, Education, Information, Sport and Budgetary Control; this was a public hearing specifically dealing with the European Schools (European Parliament 1986). Mr J.C. Thygesen, President of the Parents' Association of the Luxembourg School, stressed that were it not for the availability of a European School education for their children, neither he nor an Irish colleague would have accepted employment with the EC. Appraising the system, he held that 'for the children who succeed in the European School they are first-rate'. His colleague, Mr B. O'Brien, then president of the Parents' Association of the Brussels II School, endorsed 'their positive European and national aspects, especially the friendships ... across language and cultural barriers, resulting in mutual understanding, respect and tolerance'. While maintaining, also with qualified praise, that the system has proved itself to be a success 'at least in the case of academically gifted children', Mr O'Brien went on to criticise the Schools sharply for tolerating 'failure and attrition rates [that] would lead to a public outcry were they to occur in the national systems at home'. But there were twelve such national systems, some of which still have higher failure rates, some lower, while yet others publish no such information. Comment tends therefore to be coloured by cultural or national perspectives, and these vary widely on every major aspect of schooling.

At the same hearing, Mr Van Houtte, former chairman of the Parents' Committee in the Luxembourg School and, perhaps more than anyone else, the person who deserves the title of 'founding father' of the first European School, pointed to the 'genuine, effective participation by the teachers and parents of pupils in the management bodies, particularly the Board of Governors well beyond anything comparable in the twelve Member States'. He also quoted the report of the present writer to the Commission (Swan 1984) to the effect that 'success has been considerable'.

The European Trade Union Committee for Education (ETUCE) described the European Schools to the hearing as '... a model for the development of a feeling of intellectual solidarity in Europe [which], despite all the difficulties, makes an outstanding contribution to international understanding'.

The European Commission, on the same occasion, while admitting the need 'to ensure a balanced, non-ghetto population of the Schools' and to re-examine their organisational structure, described them as 'a unique and exciting educational experience ... which draws on the best of the national educational systems and which can enrich them [in turn]'. In short, the European Schools emerged with considerable credit, despite some hard-hitting evidence and comment, from the very close scrutiny of this two-day hearing. At the subsequent debate in the European Parliament, Mr Elliott (Socialist) summed up as follows: 'Most people ... who have looked into the European Schools regard them as necessary, and agree that they provide an excellent training on a multinational and multilinguistic basis, but they do have serious defects' (European Parliament 1986).

Towards the New Statute of 1994: the Oostlander Episode

This brings us to the European Parliament debates of 1993 and especially those related to their budget and the new Statute of 1994. A particular focus here was the Oostlander Report of June 1993, which proved to be the most radical and controversial in the series of reports on the European Schools that have been commissioned at the behest of the Parliament (Parlement Européen 1993). Fundamental issues were raised in this episode, which touched on the legal basis of these Schools and called into question their future existence, at least as we know them.

Already in 1990 the European Council and the Ministers for Education within the Council had asked for a new agreement to be drawn up for the European Schools, and they decided to consult the Parliament on this (23 March 1993). To some extent on this, as on other occasions, the Schools became an issue in the often uneasy relationship between the Parliament, the Commission and the Member States. A new Draft Statute for the European Schools was drawn up and approved by the Ministers in November 1992.

Considerable criticism of the funding of the Schools was voiced in the Parliament's Budgetary Debate in 1993, and in Mr Oostlander's Report to it (Parlement Européen 1993). The Commission drew up a memorandum which responded point by point to Mr Oostlander, and to the Parliament's amendments of the Commission's draft Statute (European Parliament, 1993). Mr Oostlander, in turn, wrote another lively document, moderating his position on some issues but scarcely on essentials (Oostlander 1993).

Mr Oostlander was strongly opposed to the Draft Statute, primarily on political and financial grounds; politically, because he distrusted inter-governmental structures as lacking accountability to parliamentary democracy, and he saw the Schools as overspending within this framework. Besides, he held, such agreements now ran counter to the principle of subsidiarity in education, which is enshrined in Article 126 of the Maastricht Treaty. In other words, he viewed the European Schools' Agreement as a 'loose cannon' on the legal deck of the European Union which should be either tied down or thrown overboard. Initially he wished to abolish the Schools, but he later modified this, proposing instead that they be integrated into the school systems of the respective countries where they are located. He also wished to adapt the Schools' curricula more clearly to the different levels of ability of the pupils; to use them to enrich the European dimension of school curricula in the national systems, make the European Baccalaureate also available in these systems, and to give all pupils in schools throughout the EU an opportunity to study a foreign language.

The Commission (European Commission 1993) calmly reminded Mr Oostlander that the Parliament's powers in the matter were advisory and supervisory, but not executive. They held that the principle of subsidiarity was not at issue here, but that what was needed was to meet shared responsibilities together; that, since the Schools exist primarily to facilitate the smooth running of the Community's institutions, a larger contribution from it (than from the Member States) to the Schools' budget was only to be expected. So in several respects, it seems, the Oostlander Report was seen as overreaching itself and perhaps as potentially exceeding, or extending, the Parliament's powers.

Now one could agree to some extent with several of the shortcomings pointed out in the Oostlander Report; for example, when it refers to the Schools as being 'isolated', asserting that they need to share their experiences more widely, and again when the report finds them expensive.

One could also agree with the report's aspiration that *all* pupils in primary schools throughout the EU ought to be given an opportunity to study a foreign language, and that the European Schools themselves should cater for pupils of a wider range of abilities. Indeed several of these same criticisms had been voiced by the present writer in his own report a decade earlier (Swan 1984). But it is not clear that Mr Oostlander had taken sufficient cognisance of the extent to which remedial measures had indeed been adopted by the Schools in the interim, as the Commission's reply to him pointed out. The extent to which they have been succeeding will emerge elsewhere in these pages, but it would be unfair to present the Schools as though they were indifferent to the need for reform.

In fact, there was a major contradiction inherent in the Oostlander recommendations, in that the proposal that the Schools be integrated into the school systems of the Member States where they are located was almost certain to deprive them of some of those unique features and experiences which marked them off as pioneering institutions whose fruits, as he pointed out, ought to be shared with other schools.

First among these would be the incommensurateness of the cultures which are represented in them. Second is the equality of esteem for each nationality which they embody, and which would be most unlikely to survive such a change. Integration would in effect amount to assimilation, and the balance of esteem which has been so carefully cultivated here, but which proves so elusive in nationally oriented schools, whether at home or abroad, would be lost. From a European point of view, this could be the greatest loss, since these Schools are successfully creating a European mentality in the view of many past pupils, including one who wrote in their defence, attacking the Oostlander proposals (Clarotti 1994). The second loss would be the equal status of two languages, the mother tongue and the *langue véhiculaire* both as prescribed and as found in the experience of each pupil, although these differ as between different groups of pupils in them. That this unique experiment *is* successful is maintained by Tosi (1991) in an interesting article in the *World Yearbook of Education* (1991), which is dealt with more fully in Chapter 2.

Again, while Oostlander seems to value some of what the Schools have achieved educationally, it is clear that the conditions stipulated in the Namur Conference Report (EEC 1990) for learning a first foreign language in primary school are more likely to be fulfilled in a European School than in its national counterparts.

As regards the charge of 'educational isolation', this too was levelled by the present writer, and it is a feature the Schools have shared with many *Auslandsschulen*. Several of the Schools (in particular Culham and Bergen), however, have been developing links with other school systems, both local and far removed. More recently, and perhaps resulting in part from the Oostlander criticisms, there is evidence that efforts in this direction have been redoubled in most Schools, e.g. in the compilation, seemingly for the first time, by the central office, of information on 'Contacts between the European Schools and the Outside World 1992-93', but no doubt more remains to be done.

Mr Oostlander's proposal that the European Baccalaureate should be made widely available in other schools, desirable though it might seem, would raise considerable problems of curriculum and staffing, and therefore of cost, for any such school. But it seems unlikely that the structure and procedures of this examination would mesh in easily with national curricula, examination procedures, and school staffing policies, in several Member States, all of which vary considerably. However, the adjustments required might be phased in at some future time, given the will to do so.

The issue of the costliness of the European Schools is dealt with below in response to a newspaper article by Marie Woolf. However, since their costs are rising sharply, while a majority of the pupils in several Schools are no longer the children of employees of European institutions, it is important to note that the fees for 'non-entitled' pupils will, following a decision of 1994, be increased by 10 per cent each year for the following ten years, although still remitted in a sizeable minority of cases where poor home circumstances obtain. Besides, the recent signing of more contracts with major employers in their vicinity will no doubt enhance the revenue from this source and place the enrolment of pupils on a more secure footing for the Schools concerned. A reduction in the number of subject options available at the senior secondary stage, as suggested by Clarotti (1994), could also reduce their costliness, but if this were to be seen as reducing the acceptability of the Baccalaureate itself internationally, it would probably be too high a price to pay.

There is no doubt that the Parliament took seriously the Oostlander criticisms and negative comments from elsewhere. Some outcomes may be noted. First is the decision that in 1995, for the first time, an observer from the Parliament will attend the meeting of the Administrative and Financial Committee on the budget of the European Schools. Besides, following a successful legal action challenging the strict implementation of the rule requiring the repatriation of teachers after nine years' secondment, the Board of Governors has established a working party to consider the Parliament's request for uniform implementation of that rule. Third, the fact that in 1993 and 1994 the Parliament has blocked the budget of the Schools is further proof of misgivings, although this can be no more than a temporary gesture.

This episode does neatly illustrate the unique political context of the European Schools, whose nearest counterpart may be the United Nations' School in New York, but even this parallel is limited. At any rate, there must have been considerable apprehensiveness and concern among the Schools' personnel throughout this debate, while any tendency towards complacency was likely to be punctured by it. But the new Statute has now been signed and is in the process of ratification by the Member States. This new lease of life must lead to increased confidence in the Schools for the future; that is, unless the Parliament still feels that the pace of change under the new Statute remains too slow and decides to intervene further.

Views of Alumni

What then are the views of those who have been through the system? Almost the only substantial published evidence on this matter comes from a questionnaire study of past pupils of one of the Schools, that in Bergen (Holland), which was carried out by three of its staff members (Blomme *et al.* 1989). Based on a response rate of approximately one-third of all the past pupils sought, 71.3 per cent of the respondents (n=105) regarded their School as 'genuinely European'. Even higher proportions commented favourably on the social contact between pupils (73.9 per cent), and the quality of the education received (72.9 per cent), while 71.2 per cent regarded it as constituting a sound basis for higher education.

Two individuals, Wathelet (1993) and Lewis (1993), both recent past pupils, committed to paper their thoughts on their European School experience. Both wrote of the 'naturalness' to them of the extraordinarily cosmopolitan, cultural 'mix' of life in a European School. Andrew Lewis found the curriculum unbalanced in favour of the academic and insufficiently oriented to art, music and sport, though 'highly positive and valuable' nevertheless. François Wathelet, on the other hand, discerned the emergence of a specifically European mentality among the pupils. He attributed this to the immensely enhanced opportunities afforded by the diversity of cultures, languages and meanings encountered within his school, and to its 'original' pedagogy of *langues véhiculaires* and European hours,[2] which both precluded prejudice and intolerance, and rendered barriers, whether of territory or of language, absurd and obsolete. Dismissing the view of a European parliamentarian who described the European School as a 'pre-historic animal', he found it, contrariwise, to offer an inspiring education and one that was ahead of its time. In other words, the 'European ideal', in his view, may be at its liveliest among some European School pupils rather than among certain European parliamentarians.

MEDIA COMMENTS

Some remaining comments on the Schools come from professional (FFPE 1991) or journalistic sources, illustrating also the widespread interest that the Schools evoke outside Europe. The former is a comment in a publication of the Fédération de la Fonction Publique Européene. Describing itself as a 'pre-sondage' carried out within the European Schools, it does make serious critical comments, based on a purported survey. However, since it presents no scientific basis for its comments, it will be disregarded here.

Jane Marshall (1987), writing in *The Times Educational Supplement* of 21 December 1987, accused the Schools of elitism, and was highly critical of overcrowding in the Brussels Schools, for which she blamed the 'excessive bureaucracy' of the system.

The charge of elitism has been reiterated elsewhere, and especially by Marie Woolf, in *The Times Educational Supplement* of 24 September 1993, and by Leonard Doyle, in *The Independent* (a British daily newspaper) of 21 April 1994. but is not found in a report by David Tytler in *The Times*, 12 January 1996.

Both writers seem to accept the Oostlander Report more or less at face value. While Doyle does quote two staff members of the School in Culham, one attacking the Schools, the other strongly supporting, and admits that the School there 'provides top class education', he goes on to add 'with a *slant* on European history, geography and culture with the objective of turning out *politically correct* European *federalists*' (emphasis added). No concession is made to the fact that Britain is physically a part of Europe and politically a member of the European Union, while the emotionally toned language in which the article is written is probably its own best criticism. A calm reply to this from Michael Ryan, a staff representative at Culham, appeared a few days later in that newspaper.

Citing Oostlander, Woolf accuses the Schools' Board of Governors of 'interfering in the everyday management of the Schools'. She also quotes a European Parliament official, Christof Wielemaker, as describing the Board of Governors as 'an uncontrollable institution', and a Labour MEP, Michael Elliott, to the effect that 'it costs more to send a child here than to Eton'.

How fair is all this comment? The present writer does not find the remark on the Board of Governors entirely consistent with his own experience. Indeed, the contrary view – that the Conseil Supérieur is too removed from the day-to-day work and reality of the Schools – has been far more frequently heard.

Second, while there is no doubt that the Schools are expensive, this is very much to be expected, and Mr Oostlander (1993) has admitted that comparison with other international, rather than with national, schools 'does place them in a far more favourable light'. This admission suggests that his initial criticism of the Schools was based on a rather superficial comparison. No other school system attempts to bear the linguistic and other curricular burdens carried by the European Schools, with teachers and pupils taken from and returning to their twelve countries of origin. The difficulty of recruiting teachers from abroad, unless salaries are made attractive, is an underlying constraint, and one which had also been adverted to in the Namur Conference Report (unpublished). No other school system has to meet twelve or fifteen separate sets of cultural and national expectations at the same time. The demands created by the structuring of these Schools into language sections means that, organisationally and financially, they resemble several schools under one roof, and comparison with the typical national school, whether public or private, is too simple. Indeed, if we look closely at the system as a whole, they comprise no less than 59 separate language sections or so many relatively separate linguistic units among them, staffed in a way that is closer to as many separate schools than to a mere nine. Added to this are the day-to-day costs of a very widely scattered network of institutions, of the harmonised curriculum across the network, the lack of suitable textbooks in many subjects, the cost of translating paperwork for administration as well as for teaching through three languages and teaching six others.

As to the comparison with Eton, one wonders does Eton use any teaching medium other than English; how many subjects will the typical student at Eton, even in sixth form, be studying at a time; and does Eton attract large numbers of qualified teachers from abroad, with non-British salary expectations? Of course other comparisons might yield different conclusions. But this comment in a journal of the standing of *The Times Educational Supplement* seems superficial and unbalanced.

On the other hand, reports on the European Schools carried in the Dutch daily newspaper *Noord Holland Dagblad* (2 and 4 April 1994), which both quoted the criticisms made by Mr Oostlander and responses to them by the Principal of the Bergen School, Mr Murphy, did so in a more detached and impartial fashion. Again the tenor of Tytler's report on the School in Culham is distinctly positive. While appraising several spects of their curriculum which 'Euro-sceptics' would find controversial, he concludes: 'The pupils' (linguistic) skill is humbling', and: 'They will receive a much more complete education than anybody else.'

Lastly, Glynn Mapes, in an article in the *Wall Street Journal* of 7 March 1990, painted a similarly favourable picture, focusing primarily on the quality, rather than the cost, of the Schools or on invidious comparison. While maintaining that the 'pan-European flavour of the Schools can cause students to lose much of their national identity and feel rootless', he also cited the present writer in stressing that they cultivate a wider view of Europe, and he summed up the system as 'a highly innovative and successful educational experiment'.

Building a European Identity

Although their founders primarily sought to meet the immediate educational needs of a specified group of children, the European Schools have from their inception embraced the ideal of cultivating a European identity as part of their *raison d'être*. This ideal is conveyed in a parchment symbolically sealed into the foundation stone of each School and originating in the Protocol to the Statute of the European Schools. It reads, in part, as follows:

> Here, while all pupils will be taught their own countries' language, literature and history by teachers from those countries, they will at the same time become accustomed from childhood to speak other languages also and absorb the combined influence of the different cultures which together make up European civilisation.
>
> Playing the same games, learning the same lessons, boys and girls of different speech and citizenship will come to know, to respect and to live in harmony with one another.

> Educated side by side, untroubled from infancy by divisive prejudices, acquainted with all that is great and good in the different cultures, it will be borne in upon them as they mature that they belong together. Without ceasing to look at their own lands with love and pride they will become in mind Europeans, schooled and ready to complete and consolidate the work of their fathers before them to bring into being a united and thriving Europe.

It is clear from this bold, idealistic set of aims, which must have seemed almost utopian at the time of its first promulgation, that the creation of a European consciousness or identity was an explicit aim from the beginning. The above statement could be interpreted as having strong undertones of both cultural nationalism and socio-political reconstructionism, but on a European scale. It could also be readily dismissed by 'Euro-sceptics' as so much 'Euro-rhetoric', designed merely to 'create an "imagined community" out of a geographical space', in the words of Philip Schlesinger (1991, p.140) writing on the analogous context of the media and Europe. He is sceptical about the 'project of Europeanisation' in that context, reaching as far back as Jean Monnet's much quoted dictum 'If we were beginning the European Community all over again, we should begin with culture', (to which 'and education' is often added by others who cite it). Schlesinger, however, dismisses this 'sacred injunction' as legitimating a kind of distortion of history, whereby we forget the devastation of Europe's past and recodify the social memory so as to construct a collective identity. If we are to achieve this, he concludes, we shall have to engage in processes of remembering what is common to European culture and society, and forget what has divided it, but also to imagine new options and possibilities (op.cit., p.178). Identity formation, he goes on, is a quest that is no longer simply a 'given', but rather a quest that is always open; individuals and groups, through their actions, participate in the formation of identity which is the result of decisions and projects, rather than conditioning and bonds (Schlesinger, quoting Melucci 1989).

Undoubtedly the question of identity itself is a crucial concern; according to the great psychoanalyst Erik Erikson (1968), it is as strategic in our time as the study of sexuality was in Freud's day. It seems to this writer, however, to result from both decisions reached *and* bonds formed. The aspiration to form or invent a European identity, therefore, in and through the European Schools, cannot be dismissed as mere rhetoric, but rather appears as education aligning itself with emergent action in response to the unfolding of European history, and this will be achieved not by distorting the past but rather by retelling honestly, especially to the children, both what has united and what has divided us.

The aspiration to educate children who will 'become in mind European' echoes the views of the founding fathers of public education in many emerging countries throughout history. For instance, Noah Webster in the post-revolutionary United States of America viewed schooling as the mould which would shape a new identity in its future citizens. At that time a separate American identity was still much more aspiration than reality among many of the colonists living 'on the edge of the howling wilderness'. A European identity was equally far to seek at the time when the first European School was established in 1953, and indeed it remains so for many, perhaps most, of the citizens of the EU countries today, more than forty years later. While these two historic aims for teachers to set before their pupils have a common element, they differ in this: that whereas the North American sets out to replace one, or alternatively many, national identities with a single one, the European sets out both to confirm existing ones and to add a supra-national layer or dimension to the national, and without diminishing it – in so far as this is possible.

But is there a danger of fostering a new kind of 'nationalism', now on a European scale, and one that could prove as pernicious at this level as its forerunners on the national scale had sometimes been found? Halls (1974) thinks not. While stressing that the Schools do not seek to 'de-nationalise' pupils, but rather to give a 'European dimension' to their education, he holds that the structure of each School into partly national, linguistic sections will ensure that they remain multinational rather than 'Euronational'. The present writer holds that their context and history to date support this viewpoint. The relatively rapid growth of the

European Union by admitting Denmark, Ireland, the UK, Greece, Spain and Portugal, as well as Finland, Sweden and Austria to membership, suggests that its guiding principles are not based on a closed mentality or on exclusiveness, but rather are inclusive and fully open to the rich contribution of internal diversity to its own identity. Following the ideals of their founders, the European Schools do emulate this inclusiveness, and indeed go to great lengths to safeguard and maintain their *separate* national identities among their pupils (e.g. by employing teachers from each of the Member States), while also permitting up to 20 per cent of the places in any class to be filled by nationals of non-EU countries.

Returning to the 1950s, it must be accepted that, with the bitter memory of two devastating World Wars still vivid in the public memory, a special responsibility devolved on educators, particularly in Europe, to work to prevent a repetition of those holocausts, both of which partly found their source in the classrooms of Europe. The socio-political reconstructionist note struck in the proclamation of the founders of the European Schools therefore sounded a warning, both historic and timely, of the need to ensure that our classrooms did not yet again support the recrudescence of extreme national antipathies.

It also received considerable moral support from the following dramatic words of Theodor W. Adorno, one of the founders of the Frankfurt School of sociology: 'That Auschwitz never happens again – this is the very first demand on education' (Adorno 1988), while recurrent outbreaks of neo-Nazism and other violent forms of extreme nationalism must still serve to dispel any complacency on the issue.

But what is most arresting is the daring of the vision which, at a time when Europe's wounds were still raw, sought not simply to restore harmony and prosperity to the individual nations of Europe, but also to work to achieve the dream of uniting these peoples culturally as well as economically, and to use the School as an agency for doing so, however small the scale of this first step.

To this extent, and while solving a practical problem for their own officials, the founders aimed also to extend the formal education of the young beyond the arena of the nation state, whose moral, political and cultural well-being were hitherto both its source and service, and to locate it in a higher plane of supranational culture and consciousness; not to supplant but to supplement local and national identities with a European one. Indeed the successive decisions of the governments concerned – to loosen the Gordian knot that had hitherto bound their national schooling so exclusively to the single parent state – deserves to be seen as a historic precedent in its own right, marking a break with the established procedure of the past and a new direction for public education in the future. In the subsequent decades we find the educational aim of creating a European identity being explicitly referred to by the EC Education Ministers in their joint statements.

Two items of evidence from empirical studies, both carried out in the European School in Bergen, relate to the matter of developing a European identity in the pupils of the European Schools. In the first one, that carried out by Blomme *et al.* (1989), it was found that 20 per cent of the *Dutch* ex-pupils responding to a questionnaire found this school 'too Dutch', while a mere 7.9 per cent of the respondents found it 'too international'. They were, after all, not in a Dutch school, but in a *European* School which happened to be in Holland! (By the way, this finding holds ironic implications for the recommendation of the Oostlander Report to the Parliament that the European Schools be integrated into the local national systems.)

The second investigation, by Bulwer (1990), an ethnographic case study of two individual pupils in their final school year, was designed to investigate how the multilingual atmosphere affects the pupils' sense of nationality and 'sense of Europeanness'. One pupil was British by birth and, following an exploration with the interviewer of her trilingualism in English, French and Dutch, she was asked 'And what do you think your nationality is now?' After a pause she answered, 'Still British, but in the direction of much more European. Yeah, European nationality, if you can talk of European nationality' (p.18).

Each of these studies illustrates in miniature not only the

loosening of identification with a single nationality that may or may not be seen as a necessary first stage in the process of 'becoming in mind European', which was the aspiration of the founders of the Schools, but also the growth of consciousness of being a citizen of Europe as well as of one's country of origin.

Quite different was the case of Wathelet (1993), whose 'Europeanness' was built not so much on top of a national identity as instead of it, though he was conscious of his mixed parental nationalities – they came from Belgium and Holland. He claims not to have realised the close identification in most others between nationality and education, until the shock of seeing this in his fellow university students caused him to notice its absence in himself! In turn this led him to realise the value of life in a European School, a 'microcosm of the living Europe' and 'une préparation véritable à la citoyenneté Européenne' (p.115).

If the development of a European identity is valued in its own right, then the unique potential of the European Schools to contribute to its growth must likewise be appreciated and valued.

SOME PROBLEMS

A school system explicitly espousing such radical aims was bound to encounter many problems. After all, in the decade in question here, twelve sovereign states were eventually to be involved as equal partners in the governance, administration and staffing of this small network of Schools. These nations have been noted as much for rivalry as for co-operation in education in the past, often taking pride in their very differences, while sometimes using these even as symbols of superiority.

Education, which is usually both a product and microcosm of a nation's history, can, more easily than most public activities, show up national differences in starkest contrast, especially when they coexist within the same school. Different nations may not share the same educational values; an apparent convergence of aim and aspiration could mask radically different ideologies of child-rearing, different mores, modes of behaviour and concepts of education. Thus it is quite surprising and encouraging to find it possible for this system to function at all, in view of its very diverse cultural sources.

Context and Challenge

The history of education in Europe is marked by competing pressures for uniformity and diversity and, again, for equality versus inequality. The first decades of existence of the European Schools in fact have witnessed unprecedented upheaval in all aspects of education in the Member States. The 'steady state' school of the past, in so far as it ever existed, changing slowly and insulated from extreme effects of the socio-political climate, has been shattered by the so-called 'explosions' in knowledge, numbers, expectations and demands. As school systems have undergone massively increased expansion and investment, the range and kinds of demand placed upon them have multiplied accordingly. Following the post-war decades of unprecedentedly rapid expansion, the more recent contraction in pupil numbers has been a further source of shock which many national school systems have had to absorb.

It was only to be expected that, sooner or later, the European Schools would encounter similar crises, if anything in a more dramatic form. Questions of what to teach (which date back to Aristotle), of how to teach it (which also confronted Quintilian), and when it should be taught, raised by Comenius and Piagetians alike, are all burning topics of today inside the European Schools, no less than without. Such problems as selective versus comprehensive admission policies, programme-centred or pupil-centred pedagogy, depth versus breadth in the curriculum, which in the past were confined to education treatises and textbooks, now crowd our newspapers. And each society or institution which establishes a public education system for the young must find its own answers, however provisional, to them. The fact that no one has provided universally acceptable answers may be disquieting or reassuring; it does compel each body to go on seeking for itself by way of research, practice and debate.

But in the case of the European Schools, such controversies

have served to heighten the challenge they already faced. By engaging teachers seconded from the several systems of the Member States, their mission was to fuse twelve school systems in microcosm into one polyglot educational community, having a new life of its own – but without severing the umbilical cords that bound them to their widely scattered origins.

Would they then become a genuine synthesis of the best thought and practice in European pedagogy, or merely a weak compromise between twelve or more national systems? Beneath a ponderous superstructure of legal, financial and administrative machinery, would there lurk competing national pedagogies – and a pecking order of leaders and led? There are critics who say that this is what has happened.

The European Schools have been compared unfavourably with the national schools which they seek in part to replicate. Perhaps the comparison is unfair, but the fact that they undertook not only to replicate them but to aim higher as well seems to have raised expectations that could scarcely ever have been fulfilled in equal measure and in all directions at the same time.

They also risk unfavourable comparison with other 'schools abroad', but these tend to look back to a single mother country and serve largely to keep its expatriate children in contact with its language, culture and institutions. This too the European Schools attempt to do, and now for fifteen nationalities at once. But again the probability is that no single institution could ever meet such diverse demands with equal success and, whereas the typical 'school abroad' tends towards the assimilation of others into its dominant culture, the European School must set its face in the opposite direction by cherishing all cultures equally.

The European Schools are presented as a kind of 'company school' to prospective employees of the EU and the other relevant institutions. Yet they fail to attract a majority even of *their* children, at least in the Brussels area. Indeed of those 'entitled' pupils who do enrol, some have to leave because of academic failure. The consequences of such departure might be tolerable to the pupil on home ground who has a local alternative at hand. But in the case of those who have none, especially those whose families have moved from Denmark, the United Kingdom, Ireland, Spain, Greece or Portugal, the effect can be shattering on themselves, on their family and its very roots. And this reality underlies some of the most vehement criticism of all.

Lastly, we have seen that European Schools were intended to forge a new dimension of identity for Europeans of the future. Schools have always been required to find some equilibrium between tradition from the past and change for the future. Frequently they may have been able to build upon a relatively stable consensus of values in the culture they sought to transmit, though this is often less clear today. But the teacher in the European School, even more than his or her colleagues at home, has no single set of such values as a source, but rather a largely post-Christian and post-industrial plurality of perspectives, at best a post-modern and singular pluralism, in philosophical terms. This, of course, probably reflects in some degree the reality of what is taking place in the teacher's home country anyhow, though such stated philosophies can also be at odds with its reality.

On the individual level, the vocation of the teacher in the European School is still the balanced development of the young. On the social level it is either a commitment to fifteen nationalities at once or to a unified, multinational society still to be born. Politically it is to a future aspiration as much as to a tangible reality. Culturally it may be to a creative pluralism, a radical eclecticism, or to a multilingual, multiethnic and multi-confessional Europe. His only certainty is either rooted in what remains of the established past, or in the uncertainty of future change itself. Legislators do not always realise that teachers must work in the present, with whatever is to hand, including the contradictions and conflicts of the adult society which they must confront in their teaching, a reality that has been too easily overlooked in the Oostlander Report. Despite these conflicts and constraints, many teachers in the European Schools are doing a superb job achieving at the individual level what neither the Treaties of Rome nor of Maastricht dared to initiate at the international level.

CONCLUSION

The foregoing gives some idea of the context of time, place and thought of the European Schools. It is doubtful whether a school system anywhere has been charged with so daunting a task. Achievement can be assessed only in relation to expectation, but here the expectations themselves often fail to harmonise, and frequently compete with each other.

How successful, then, are the European Schools in achieving their very ambitious politico-social aims, and at the same time in meeting the basic educational needs of their target population?

First, the 'European ideal' is now reaching fruition in the emerging mentality of many of their pupils and past pupils. Unlike their parents, these young persons are fluent in three or even four languages. They 'think European', are much less susceptible to national myths and stereotypes, and develop a concept of national differences that is far more mature than that of their fellow Europeans at home.

Second, as pioneers of the very concept of equality of esteem among different national groups, with the emphasis on plurality rather than assimilation, and challenging the commitment of governments and parents alike to modify extreme forms of nationalism in education, they are also succeeding.

Third, the past pupils of the European Schools have already established a fine reputation for them among universities throughout Europe, thus extending the widespread acceptance of their Baccalaureate among diverse and sceptical institutions.

But this success is costly. First, they are failing to attract many of those children whom the Schools seek most to serve. Second, they are rejecting a number of those whom they do admit. And lastly, like all types of international schools, they incur an understandably far greater cost per pupil than is usual in the national school systems of the Member States.

Their crucial academic problem is this – how to balance the maintenance of the highest possible academic standards with the most comprehensive rates of access and retention, at least among 'entitled' pupils, as long as this status applies.

Chapter 2

CURRICULUM AND ASSESSMENT: ELIDING FOREIGNNESS

> Europe is a complex ... whose proper function is to assemble the largest possible diversity without confounding it, to associate contraries while safeguarding their separateness.
>
> Edgar Morin

> It is a shame and bad taste to be an alien, and it is no use pretending otherwise. There is no way out of it. A criminal may improve and become a decent member of society. A foreigner cannot improve. Once a foreigner, always a foreigner.
>
> Humorist George Mikes (1946)

Given the simultaneously national and European orientations of the European Schools, is their curriculum a genuine synthesis of the best, or merely the lowest common denominator to which none of the Member States objects? Are we witnessing cultural fusion or confusion? The answers – for there will be more than one – lie partly in the history of the Schools, partly in their antecedent cultural differences and kinships, and partly in the mind of the beholder. After all, what kind of curriculum could possibly be designed to meet the needs of children from twelve sovereign countries, with nine major languages, and on the basis of equality among them, despite the fact that curricular frameworks tend to be surprisingly similar from country to country?

Within the relatively homogeneous culture of a single Member State, a process of cultural analysis, such as that proposed by Lawton (1989), could help towards devising a curriculum suitable for that culture. However, despite its deep roots and common origins, Europe is by no means a homogeneous cultural entity; in the European Schools' context, where so many languages and cultures converge and where terms as basic as *culture* (French), *Bildung* (German), *pegagogia* (Italian) and *education* (English) almost defy precise translation, what is needed is a pluralistic, cross-cultural analysis, at least to indicate points of departure. It is also needed because teachers teach and parents raise their children in the ways they do, not just as a result of rationally choosing one among many options, but mainly as they have been influenced by their own upbringing, their own educational, cultural and linguistic origins. And each of these diverse ways can come to be seen as self-evidently the 'right' or the only acceptable one, despite the fact that what is unthinkable in one country's schools may be commonplace in another's; in short, 'Eurocentrism' or a sense of 'alternativism' (see Nordenbo 1993) with regard to one's own curricula and culture exists, as yet, in few of the Member States' schools.

The Tapestry of Curricula in EU Member States

The harmonised syllabus of the European Schools did not take shape *in vacuo* but began with a Community comprising the six founding Member States – Belgium, France, Germany, Italy, Luxembourg and the Netherlands, with their four official languages and the considerable common ground between their curricula. At the same time the syllabus was shaped by the reconstructionist aims shared by all six, set forth in the foundation document.

It was shaped as well by the pressing need to educate the

children of a large number of expatriate families, in widely scattered centres. The accession to membership of the United Kingdom, Denmark and Ireland, followed later by Greece, Spain and Portugal, all provided new challenges, 'distant air and the supply of new blood', in the words of Thomas Mann (see Opitz 1990).

Different cultural patterns had of course existed historically long before the national school systems emerged which would serve mainly to select and carry them forward. These came into awareness as fundamental differences in curricular philosophy and ideology, and especially in attitudes to knowledge or notions of what knowledge is of most worth, as between European school systems. The following very simplified typology given by McLean (1990) helps to illustrate the distribution of major traditions:

1. The 'encyclopaedic heartlands' (France, Italy, Spain, Portugal, Belgium and Luxembourg).
2. The (classical) 'humanist periphery' (England and Wales, Greece and Ireland; Scotland and Northern Ireland 'with qualification').
3. The 'naturalist variations' (Germany, the Netherlands, Denmark).

These terms are seen not as offering either pure colours or a full spectrum of curricular traditions, but rather as templates against which dominant patterns may be discerned. All of them have distinct cultural meanings, along with somewhat different notions of what knowledge is of most value, and different attitudes to the roles of the student and teacher, while each constitutes a relatively separate pattern within the tapestry.

Encyclopaedism, originating in pre-revolutionary France, is associated with transmitting a broad range of rational, codified knowledge to pupils who must be mature enough to absorb it. Cultivating breadth of knowledge and rationality are major curricular aims; the very broad curriculum, as well as the study of philosophy at school level in many continental countries and the European Schools themselves, may illustrate these aims.

Humanism, with its classical origins, focuses on depth rather than breadth of knowledge (as in the British A-levels) and more on developing the person than transmitting the culture, but, like encyclopaedism, it too can lead to elitist forms of schooling.

As distinct from these, the naturalist approach, which is more a pedagogy than an epistemology, takes more clearly into account the processes of child development and learning, and insists on adapting curricular content to these. It also places a greater emphasis on democratic values (e.g. parental involvement in schooling) than the others do.

In fact none of these three curricular traditions exists exclusively or in undiluted form in any of the countries in question. Nevertheless, they have had a major influence on them historically. Research by Broadfoot *et al.*, comparing French with British teachers, seems to support this typology by finding that 'the French teachers were more concerned with cognitive outcomes than their British counterparts, who tended to put more emphasis on the whole child...' rather than on academic achievement (Broadfoot *et al.* 1988), while it may be no harm to recall that 'every culture always interprets other cultures within its own framework' (Nordenbo 1993, p.20).

Application to the European Schools' Curriculum

How then might we apply this template to understanding the European Schools' curriculum? When the Department of Education and Science in London describes them as being 'comparable with the French Lycée or the German Gymnasium' (Department of Education and Science 1985), when a British parent describes them as 'quite Napoleonic', when an Irish teacher holds that 'French pupils consider the teacher as a being apart from their world' (McGrath 1982), or a German teacher maintains that the British brought with them a lot of 'team spirit' (Opitz 1990) – then each commentator must be understood as selecting one aspect of the Schools which strikes him as 'different', while betraying also the commentator's point of view. The templates of the perceiver may be discerned behind many of the comments, both private and public, which one has heard on the European Schools.

A Singular Pluralism

Yet, according to Hart (1992), 'nearly everything in a European School represents a compromise between the twelve different Member States: the timetables and the holidays, the class sizes and the teachers' weekly teaching load, the criteria for promotion and the marking and evaluation systems'. Nevertheless, the lessons are not identical from one language section to another, and 'pupils have the benefit of experiencing different teaching styles' (ibid., p.30).

Beneath apparent similarities, e.g. in prescribed syllabi, there can be wide disparities of pedagogy, expectations and demands on pupils, while different European traditions or *rites de passage* through school seem to distinguish rather clearly among our school systems. For instance, according to published (though incomplete) data for the years 1975-80 (International Bureau of Education 1983), the incidence of grade repetition was highest in the schools of France and Italy, followed by Holland and Germany, with England and Denmark seemingly among the lowest of the monolingual EC Member States of the time.

In 1984 the present writer computed the rank order of the incidence of grade repetition, aggregated across all the corresponding language sections of the European Schools for the years 1978 to 1983, as shown in Table 2.1. This was then compared statistically with the national data from those countries, and the resulting rank order correlation coefficient value of r = .76 suggested a high correspondence between the two sets of data (Swan 1984).

Table 2.1 Mean Failure Rate across Language Sections of the Combined European Schools 1978-83

Language Section	French	Italian	Dutch	German	English	Danish
% $\bar{M}$ Rate	8.97	8.72	6.55	5.53	5.06	3.04
Rank	1	2	3	4	5	6

This study was then brought up to date by scrutinising the failure rates in the European Baccalaureate (which had been found in turn to correspond to those in the lower grades of the Schools) for the years 1989-92. They showed a striking, though not perfect, persistence of the same rank order from the previous decade among the language sections across all nine schools (Board of Governors of the European Schools 1993), as illustrated in Table 2.2.

Table 2.2 Failure Rate by Language Section in the European Schools: Rank Order for Each Year

Language Section	1989	1990	1991	1992	Mean Rank
French	3	2	1	1	1.75
Italian	1	4	2	2	2.25
Dutch	2	3	3	3	2.75
English	4	5	4	4	4.25
Danish	6	1	6	5	4.50
German	5	6	5	6	5.50

It can be seen from Table 2.2 that the highest mean rank (signifying the highest failure rate) was still occupied by the French language section, and the examiners concluded that in 1992 'it was more difficult to obtain a good Baccalaureate in the French section than in others'. They were followed by the Italian, with the Danish second lowest and the German lowest, across the four-year span.

It is interesting to note that the sequence in Table 2.2 corresponds fairly closely to McLean's typology in the following order: encyclopaedist – humanist – naturalist, grouping the French and Italians together at one end (encyclopaedist), the Danes and Germans together at the other (naturalist), the English (humanist) in the middle, with only the Dutch departing from the expected order.

To sum up, the rank order of different national idioms or underlying traditions of education, as expressed in examination results, showed a rather close correspondence between the national school systems and the (most nearly) corresponding language sections in the European Schools; their rank order also remained remarkably stable from decade to decade within the Schools, including their categorisation within the typology developed by McLean. National differences in idioms of schooling die hard, it seems!

Yet it is not intended to place too much emphasis on differences here – the actual raw percentage success rates were all between 87 and 97 per cent – since all these European traditions share much common ground with each other and with the newer Member States of Greece, Spain and Portugal. Besides, there is some recent evidence of convergence between language sections in the finding that the average Baccalaureate mark in Geography in 1994 was identical as between the anglophone and the francophone pupils across all the Schools, although these were taught through a second language, a different one in each case (Galvin 1995). However, one might hazard a description of the unified, harmonised curricula of the European Schools today as having an encyclopaedist base, with strong humanist and naturalist ingredients, and a reconstructionist flavour.

But it would be mistaken to assume that the common syllabus of the European Schools has remained static throughout their forty years' existence. Indeed, since 1974 a Reform Committee has played a most important role in bringing forward fresh thinking from the teachers, inspectors and parents, suggesting a considerable fermentation in fundamental notions of curriculum across the nationalities in question. In its first sixteen years the Reform Committee had presented no less than 30 documents which were adopted by the Board of Governors, dealing with issues ranging from subject-matter content and extra-curricular activities to the Schools' internal structures. But before looking at reforms, a brief description of the syllabus itself is required.

School Organisation: Levels of Study

The usual duration of primary and secondary schooling combined, however structured, in the twelve EU Member States in question is twelve or thirteen years. With this in mind, it was decided to structure the primary programme in the European Schools over a five-year period, the secondary to last seven years.

In each of the schools the kindergarten section enrols children between the ages of three and six, in theory in the language section that corresponds (most closely) to the individual's mother tongue. In practice it is not always easy to determine precisely which is the child's dominant language, owing, for instance, to frequent international relocation of the family during early childhood, to complex linguistic backgrounds caused by parental remarriage, or to multilingual households. Even at this level, a School may comprise up to seven language sections, although a problem may arise later when the range of language sections is less extensive in the kindergarten than in the primary school. A useful and wide-ranging report on Nursery Education was produced by the Reform Committee and adopted by the Board of Governors in September 1983 (Husband 1983). It placed this facet of the European Schools' curriculum usefully in the context of current thinking, and set the tone for future developments.

Primary Level

The primary level pupil spends most of the week – between 25.5 hours and 27.25 hours – in the language section chosen (see Table 2.3). From the beginning he is taught a second language, which is untypically early, whether by the standards of national or international schools; it exists, however, in Ireland, Belgium and Luxembourg.

This second or vehicular language must be different from that of the section in which the pupil is enrolled and, while not the same for everyone, it must be one of English, French or German. First learned as a subject, it will, from third year onwards, become the medium of instruction and of communication among pupils for a limited range of subjects, as Table 2.3 shows. Thus two syllabi exist for each of these three languages, the first as mother tongue, the second as a second language.

Based on a careful comparison of the national curricula, a harmonised curriculum has been worked out which seeks to be

A Singular Pluralism

Table 2.3 Primary School Programme

1st and 2nd years	No. of hours	No. of lessons
L1 (mother tongue as a subject)	8 hours	16 x 30 mins
Mathematics	4 hours	8 x 30 mins
L2 (second language) vehicular language as a subject	2.5 hours	5 x 30 mins
Music	1.5 hours	3 x 30 mins
Art	2 hours	4 x 30 mins
Physical Education	2 hours	4 x 30 mins
Environmental studies (History, Geography, Science)	1 hour	2 x 30 mins
Religion or Ethics	1 hour	2 x 30 mins
Recreation	3.5 hours	7 x 30 mins
Total	25.5 hours	51 x 30 mins
3rd, 4th and 5th Years		
L1 as a subject	6.75 hours	9 x 45 mins
Mathematics	5.25 hours	7 x 45 mins
L2 vehicular language as a subject	3.75 hours	5 x 45 mins
Environmental studies (History, Geography, Science)	3 hours	4 x 45 mins
Art	0.75 hours	1 x 45 mins
Music	0.75 hours	1 x 45 mins
Physical Education (vehicular language)	0.75 hours	1 x 45 mins
European hours (vehicular language)	2.25 hours	3 x 45 mins
Religion or Ethics	1.5 hours	2 x 45 mins
Recreation	2.5 hours	
Total	27.25 hours	33 x 45 mins

identical in all the several language sections across the Schools, and to reach identical standards in L1 (mother tongue), Mathematics, and L2 (*langue véhiculaire*). Once they have been agreed by negotiation between the national experts, the syllabi are then promulgated by the Board of Governors, which must approve any amendments.

The Mathematics syllabus is based on a modern approach and has some printed textbooks, unlike certain other subjects whose numbers are too small to repay printing costs. Known as 'Euro-maths', these textbooks ingeniously present the course through diagrams, drawings and mathematical symbols, thus bypassing language differences. They could by the same token underplay the role of problem-solving in mathematics, however, unless supplemented by other teaching materials.

Environmental studies includes History, Geography and aspects of Science at a suitable level. History begins with 'how people lived' in earlier times, and goes on to focus on the lives of major personalities in human history, deliberately seeking to avoid inculcating or transmitting nationally biased attitudes to historical events. The difficulties encountered in teaching this subject through L1 and of defining its objectives have been discussed in an interesting way by Opitz (1990) and by Van der Spek (1994).

In Geography, the syllabus concentrates first on the country in which they are living, although this must surely challenge those new teachers, always a large majority, who come from abroad. It goes on to deal with the general elements of the subject, with the aid of materials assembled from the Member States. The regulation requires that the geography of the pupil's own country be dealt with in detail.

It will be seen from Table 2.3, which presents a skeleton timetable, that in the course of the week the junior primary school pupil spends at least 2.5 hours in the environment of a language other than his or her mother tongue, while in the senior primary grades this increases to over six hours weekly. For linguistically weaker pupils, and for latecomers to the School, this could prove to be too much, despite the fact that this second language must be taught by means of a 'communicative' approach and in the *oral* form only, up to fourth grade. The fact that foreign language teaching takes place not in separate language sections but in classes of mixed nationalities and mother tongues, added to the possibility that teachers at this level will not be language specialists and may not have had training in teaching their mother tongue as a foreign language, adds to the burden, again weighing most heavily on the less gifted pupils.

Therefore, the basic structure of separate language sections

A Singular Pluralism

in each primary school, essential though it is, could give rise to some serious problems, especially in smaller language sections. These may be exacerbated by the plurality of national backgrounds within a given class, the high incidence of new admissions and departures throughout the year, the absence of kindergarten facilities corresponding to all language sections, and the combination of pupils from several grade levels into the same class, owing to small numbers. This combination itself can increase the daily frequency of coming and going of pupils who must leave their classroom for such lessons as European Hours and Ethics/Religion classes, thus fragmenting the continuity and cohesiveness of the week's work early in the pupil's career.

Apart from divergent approaches to teaching reading, which will derive both from methodological and cultural differences (e.g. as between highly phonetic and aphonetic languages), an unresolved problem arises from the different handwriting scripts which a pupil encounters. These also originate in European cultural differences, as well as the fact that different scripts are associated with each of the two different languages a pupil is learning, at this stage. In theory, the teacher is required to avoid imposing any particular style, yet it is only by avoiding the use of either the chalkboard or the handwritten word that this can be done. This is a considerable problem when teaching handwriting itself; it is exacerbated by the heavy dependence on handouts, necessitated by the dearth of suitable textbooks in the various languages used.

The 'European Hour' (actually of 45 minutes duration) which is a thrice-weekly feature of the timetable from third grade primary to fifth, is unique to the European Schools. Conducted in a second language, which may or may not be the L2 chosen by some pupils, it illustrates the seriousness with which the fusing of different nationalities is taken (Ó Néill 1990). Here pupils are regrouped into classes of about 20, of mixed nationality and/or mother tongue, in order to help them deliberately to break down linguistic and social barriers, while learning arts, crafts, cooking and physical education, through co-operative activities. While the aim is indeed praiseworthy, the reality is that the teacher may communicate in one language, while the pupils speak to each other in one or more different languages; sometimes, indeed, the teacher may not have any language in common with some of the pupils, resulting in problems of control and little learning. Though generally accepted as an important innovation in theory, the practice of the 'European Hour' was called into question by the Reform Committee in 1980 and again by the primary inspectorate in 1984.

Remedial Teaching

Following repeated representations, including those made in the present writer's 1984 report, six years' discussion at Board of Governors level, and a limited trial period in one School, it was decided in principle in 1984 to extend remedial teaching to all the primary schools. One teacher per language section would be released, as far as possible, to undergo appropriate training.

Both the resistances which may be inferred from the time lag in introducing it, and the experiences encountered in its operation, provide an interesting vignette of the variety of attitudes to this concept in the national systems. To some it was new and, one may say, rather suspect; to others it was already in operation at home and was taken for granted as an integral part of their school system. Some argued that such a support service would be unnecessary, given the affluent background of the typical European Schools' pupil, no doubt assuming that learning difficulties have only socio-economic causes.

However, in the event, it emerged that a sizeable proportion of these pupils, like pupils in any system, did indeed have learning difficulties which needed additional expert attention. The most common difficulty was with the language of instruction, caused or aggravated by interruptions in schooling. Frequent family movement caused problems of confused cultural identity or of adjustment to new school systems and media of instruction, while marital breakdown and a high incidence of single-parent families were also found to be associated with school problems. In particular, children who were placed in a language section other than that of their mother tongue contributed substantially to the occurrence of learning difficulties.

In 1989 the Board of Governors decided to admit a small number of children with a mental or physical disability – though a very few were already enrolled. This scheme, as well as the deployment of remedial teachers, has been reviewed and on the whole has been regarded as highly satisfactory, especially owing to the strong support of school administrations and the enthusiastic professionalism of the teachers. It does require close liaison with the para-educational services available from outside the School. It also requires close teacher collaboration, and it is interesting to note that in the early years of its operation a varied influence of national backgrounds was found in that in some language sections there was little or no contact between the remedial teachers and the pupils' class teacher, whereas in others this was readily established. An exclusive preoccupation with cognitive functioning also hampered progress in some sections, whereas an approach to teaching which balanced the cognitive, the affective and the psychomotor characterised the remedial teachers' approaches in other sections.

To sum up, the primary departments of the European Schools offer the unique advantages of cultural and linguistic richness, side by side with continuing contact with the home country's school system through compatriot teachers, and the facility to rejoin it should the need arise. Despite the heavy linguistic burden and the fragmentation of the pupils' weekly experience, the primary schools do provide learning environments which have many happy pupils. However, they did inherit a programme-centred quality with some inbuilt rigidities, which were seen by many as outmoded and were already disappearing from some national systems themselves.

SECONDARY LEVEL

The secondary stage of schooling lasts seven years, from ages 11 to 18. It is sub-divided into the Observation Period (three years), Pre-Orientation (two years), and the Orientation Period (years 6 and 7). Pupils still remain grouped in their language sections throughout their secondary years. When a class becomes too large (i.e. over 32 pupils), it is divided, but pupils are not combined, for this purpose, across language sections.

Promotion of the pupil from primary to secondary level is a matter for decision by a committee comprising the head teacher, the deputy head and the teachers of the 5th class primary; regulations stipulate that pupils who have passed out of the primary are normally admitted to the secondary school.

Observation Period

The aims of the observation period, according to decisions reached by the Board of Governors in 1990, include the consolidation of work already done, alleviating difficulties encountered, and helping the pupil towards greater independence and responsibility.

During the observation period, all pupils share a common stream and follow the compulsory core of subjects as follows (see Table 2.4): mother tongue (L1), basic Mathematics, *langue véhiculaire* (L2), Human Sciences (History and Geography), Natural Sciences and Technology, Latin or Graphic Arts or Music, Physical Education, Religion or Ethics, and Complementary Activities (musical/artistic/technical – optional) in years 2 and 3. A third language (L3) – one of the seven official EU languages – is begun in year 2, as shown in Table 2.4.

All subjects are taught through L1, except those noted in Table 2.4 as 'vehicular Ls'. Human Sciences (History and Geography) are taught through the medium of L1 in Years 1 and 2, but in the vehicular language (L2) in Year 3. Besides Graphic and Plastic Arts, Music and Physical Education, as well as Complementary Activities, may be taught through a second language, thus increasing the weekly amount of teaching not given in the mother tongue up to age fifteen.

While the language teaching strategies in the Schools vary from traditional to communicative, there is no doubt that the pupils' motivation is greatly helped by the polyglot environment

A Singular Pluralism

Table 2.4 Programme for the First Three Years in Secondary School: the Observation Cycle

Subject	1st Year Lessons of 45 minutes	2nd Year Lessons of 45 minutes	3rd Year Lessons of 45 minutes
L1 as a subject	6	5	4
Mathematics	4	4	4
L2 vehicular language as a subject	5	4	4
L3 as a subject (a)	–	3	3
Latin (optional)	–	–	(4)
Human Sciences (b)	3	3	3
Integrated Science	4	4	4
Graphic and Plastic Arts (vehicular languages) (c)	2	2	(2)
Music (vehicular languages) (c)	2	2	(2)
Physical Education (vehicular languages)	3	3	3
Religion or Ethics	2	2	2
Complementary Activities (vehicular languages) (d)	1	(2)	(2)
Total weekly periods (with selection of subjects in Years 2 and 3)	32	32	31 or 33

(a) Pupils may choose from among the nine official languages one which they have not yet studied; in smaller schools, their choice will be more restricted.
(b) Taught through the medium of the vehicular L2 in the 3rd year.
(c) Pupils who take Latin may discontinue either Graphic and Plastic Arts or Music.
(d) Pupils must choose two out of the range of activities offered in the first year, but Complementary Activities are optional in the second and third years.

of the School, which seems to overcome the inhibitions about risk-taking that so often dominate the language learner in monoglot environments.

The pupils do learn a great deal from each other here, especially in the large number of lessons taught in the vehicular language, as well as in Physical Education and Art, where they may rub shoulders with their fellows from any language section.

The weekly number of lessons in the mother tongue was increased from five to six in 1990. The increase was needed because (i) pupils living abroad can sometimes have a rather tenuous hold on their mother tongue, especially if their parents speak different languages, and (ii) the L1 groups in the Schools may include a variety of national and linguistic groups whose grasp of this language itself varies widely. This argues the need to extend remedial teaching to the secondary departments of the Schools.

From third year on, Human Sciences (History and Geography) are taught in the *langue véhiculaire* (L2) in which pupils will have varying degrees of proficiency. To some extent an interdisciplinary approach is used to enable them to discover the interaction of History and Geography throughout human history, while individual research, beginning from one's immediate surroundings, is officially encouraged. Again language limitations must inhibit those aspects of such enquiry as would bring the pupil into contact with the social environment of the School, in the case of many pupils. The great disadvantage in teaching such subjects in a language other than the mother tongue is that, instead of lessons in History or Geography, they can really become language lessons (Van der Spek 1994), thus calling into question educational priorities.

In Regional Geography, special attention is paid to the countries of the EU through such themes as urban and rural habitats, farming patterns, energy supply, traffic and trade routes. Greater attention needs to be focused, however, on the local geography of the outlying regions of the Union, and on extending the pupil's interest in the geography and history of his homeland, not only when this is a central, but especially when it is a peripheral region of the European Union. There also seems to be a lack of consultation with the primary teachers which would ensure continuity in the pupils' learning.

For History teaching, groups are formed across language sections, which means that children of various nationalities work together. Teaching History to non-compatriots may well compel the teacher to question assumptions which never needed questioning on home ground, in order to ensure that the standpoint taken is free of national bias. Teachers freely admit the value of this in causing them to revise assumptions they may have held in the past. It also casts both national and international issues in a new light, although a sort of centripetal tendency might well also lead here to the neglect of the study of local history for its own sake, especially if the selection and presentation of topics is to be made in the light of 'central' influence and importance only.

Mathematics is taught for four lessons weekly in the observation period, and again is based on a 'modern mathematics' approach, aligned to the most demanding syllabus requirements of the Member States. It is designed to bring out the basic unity of mathematical studies, rather than keeping Algebra, Geometry and Elementary Analysis in separate, watertight compartments. The teaching seeks to be inductive in the lower forms, beginning with everyday experience and only gradually becoming deductive. Teaching methods are harmonised across the seven language sections.

For the first three years also, science subjects are not separated but are combined, as is usual elsewhere, into a single subject known as 'Integrated Science', covering Biology and elementary ideas of Physics and Chemistry. The writer has seen some marvellous Biology work being done on the flora and fauna of the region, in European Schools.

It will be noted also from Table 2.4 that in the secondary, as in the primary, timetable, two hours weekly are given to teaching Religion or Ethics. This is in line with the principle enunciated in Article 4 of the Statute that the conscience and convictions of individuals will be respected. However, it will not be enough to prepare a pupil for the specialised study of this subject after leaving school.

The objectives of the syllabus of the observation period are excellent, enshrining ideals which remain as valid in principle and as relevant today as when they first gained currency in France and elsewhere during the 1960s. This period coincides with the stage of human development during which the first differences between inclinations and abilities begin to manifest themselves. The pupil should begin now to discover and reflect on her strengths and weak points and, with help from teachers and parents alike, to accept a growing personal responsibility for her own scholastic progress as well as for personal behaviour.

But it is feared that these objectives are achieved only to a limited extent in the European Schools, whether for reasons that derive from cultural and national differences in pedagogy, from remote bureaucratic control or from personalities. High rates of pupil failure, added to inadequately developed guidance and pastoral care structures, and the absence of remedial teaching at this level to date, are seen as relevant here.

The Pre-Orientation Cycle (Years 4 and 5)

Commencing in their fourth year, each pupil's curriculum becomes partly differentiated by the availability of options to be chosen. In the fourth and fifth years, as Table 2.5 shows, the weekly number of class periods of courses common to all pupils is 27 or 29, depending on whether one chooses a four- or a six-period Mathematics course. This structure, illustrated in Table 2.5, is made up of the common core plus six to eight elective subjects, from which the pupil will choose a sufficient number to ensure that her total timetable reaches between 31 and 35 periods weekly. All subjects are taught through L1, except those indicated by vehicular Ls in the Table 2.5. Language lessons are now given across whole-year groups, i.e. pupils combine for these, irrespective of what language section they belong to.

The possibility of taking a fourth language (L4), as well as Ancient Greek and Economic and Social Sciences, now arises. Civic and Social Education enter into both History and Geography at this point. The Natural Sciences divide into Physics, Chemistry and Biology, with two periods each, while the Human Sciences revert to separate History and Geography lessons with equal time allocations. The number of subjects now studied will seem excessive to some parents; to others it will seem quite natural.

The linguistically able and ambitious pupil will have a rich diet

Table 2.5   Programme for the Pre-orientation Cycle of Secondary School, 4th and 5th Years

Common core subjects	4th & 5th years 45-minute sessions
Religion	1
L1 as a subject	4
L2 vehicular language as a subject	3
L3 as a subject	3
Physical Education (vehicular languages)	2
History (vehicular languages)	2
Geography (vehicular languages)	2
Biology	2
Chemistry	2
Physics	2
Mathematics	4 or 6
Elective Subjects	
L4 as a subject	4
Latin	4
Greek	4
Economics and Social Sciences (vehicular Ls or the language of the host country)	4
Plastic Arts (vehicular languages)	2
Music (vehicular languages)	2
Total weekly timetable	Minimum 31 periods Maximum 35 periods

now, with the possibility of choice from among six languages (two ancient and four modern), and up to 22 language lessons weekly. The reduction from six to four periods for mother tongue now seems to reach the very minimum acceptable, especially in view of its possibly weak grasp among expatriate pupils. The curriculum, crowded though it now is, does maintain a balance, since even the most committed linguist must still take Natural Sciences and Mathematics as well as History and Geography.

THE INTERMEDIATE EVALUATION

Both the heavily academic orientation of the curriculum and the mobility of many of the pupils have long been seen as arguments for an alternative award to the Baccalaureate, and at an earlier point in the pupil's schooling, which might be critically important for the future career of early leavers. Such an alternative has long been available in most of the Member States. Table 2.6 illustrates these, and parents from many countries have demanded this facility.

Table 2.6   Existing Equivalents to Intermediate Certificate Examination in some Member States

Belgium	Certificat de l'enseignement secondaire inférieur/ Certificaat van het Lager Middelbaar Onderwijs
France	Certificat de fin de scolarité du 1er cycle Admission, après examen d'entrée éventuel, dans les établissements d'enseignement technique
Germany	Abschlusszeugnis der Realschule/Mittlere Reife
Ireland	Junior Certificate
Italy	1. Diploma di 'Applicato ai servizi amministrativi' rilasciato dagli Istituti Professionali a corso biennale 2. Ammissione all'Istituto Professionale o Diploma Istituti Professionali Biennali 3. Ammissione all'Istituto Tecnico dopo un esame (Istituto Tecnico Commerciale o Industriale, 3° anno, a seconda che siano state studiate le materie facoltative del 1° o del 2° gruppo dei 'Corsi a scelta')
Luxembourg	1. Collège d'enseignement moyen, fin de division inférieur 2. Ecoles professionnelles
Netherlands	M.A.V.O. IV
United Kingdom	GCE O-levels/General Certificate of Secondary Education

In 1988 the Board of Governors approved the creation of an Intermediate evaluation and certificate in the European Schools to be compulsory for all pupils. Based on the syllabi of years 4 and 5, it would comprise oral and written examinations in five of the subjects/areas of the syllabus. Although scheduled for introduction in 1991/92, it was only in 1994 that this procedure was introduced; it still awaits recognition in the Member States.

The Orientation Cycle (6th and 7th Years)

The orientation cycle is the final phase of schooling. During it, decisions must be reached on the pupil's future, and educational authorities in certain Member States ensure that professional career guidance personnel are available to their pupils in the Schools. Distances from home universities and difficulty in obtaining up-to-date information are two problems to be overcome in this year, apart from many young school-leavers feeling uncertain about a chosen career.

Although the number of compulsory subjects is now, on entry to sixth year, reduced from eleven to nine, the syllabus for these two years comes even more to resemble the continental European model, both in its exclusively academic bias and its very broad range of subjects, as Table 2.7 illustrates.

In view of the historical origins of the Schools and of the breadth of their own curriculum at this stage in most Member States, the fact that it is so broad here will not be surprising to most parents other than those from England, Wales and Northern Ireland. In fact in Scotland and Ireland and in the remaining Member States, it may range between seven (in the former) and 14 (in Germany for instance). Here the issue of breadth versus depth (deriving from encyclopaedism versus humanism, presumably) is at its most acute. Yet other issues, such as the need for balance and the undesirability of too early specialisation, especially at a time when young persons may change their mind frequently, and with at least two or more changes of one's later adult career now becoming a common occurrence – all seem to argue in favour of a broad curriculum at what is fast becoming

Table 2.7 Programme for the Final Two Years of Secondary Education: the Orientation Cycle

Compulsory Subjects		6th and 7th Years (45-minute sessions)
L1 as a subject		4
L2 vehicular language as a subject		3
Philosophy		2
Mathematics		3 or 5
Biology		2
History (vehicular languages)		2
Geography (vehicular languages)		2
Physical Education		2
Religion or Ethics		1
Total	minimum	21
	maximum	23

Elective Subjects (a) (of which two must be chosen)

Latin	4
Greek	4
Economics (vehicular languages or language of host country)	4
Physics	4
Chemistry	4
Biology	4
L3 as a subject	4
L4 as a subject	4
Advanced course in L1 as a subject	3
Advanced in vehicular L2 as a subject	3
Advanced course in Mathematics	3

Additional Subjects (b)

Advanced course in Geography (vehicular languages)	2
Advanced course in History (vehicular languages)	2
Plastic Arts (vehicular languages)	2
Music	2
Sociology	2
Physics and Chemistry	2
Other subjects	2

(a) The pupil's timetable must have a minimum of 31 and a maximum of 35 periods.
(b) Additional courses can be dispensed with if pupils have a minimum of 31 periods after choosing at least two elective subjects.

the final stage of basic schooling for most pupils.

Reverting to the European Schools' curricular content, as Table 2.7 shows, Philosophy is now added in sixth year and is a compulsory subject for the remaining two years, receiving between four and six periods weekly. It is a long-established subject in the senior curriculum in France where it remains compulsory in the final Lycée class for all pupils. It is also well established in Germany, Italy, Spain, Portugal and Greece. In the European Schools, the Philosophy syllabus is so designed as to cover the major schools of thought and methods of approach, but without much emphasis on, or reference to, original texts.

Economics continues as an elective subject, while the insistence on teaching it through the *langue véhiculaire*, unless it is taught in the language of the country where the School is located, is justified on the grounds that its technical nomenclature is more or less international anyhow. Sociology is introduced as an option at this stage, as in some countries (e.g. Germany and the UK) but, unlike the latter, Psychology is not available in the European Schools.

The teaching of History and Geography through a foreign language at this final stage of schooling is a vexed question. While a high level of proficiency can usually be expected in that medium by now, the issue of whether thinking at one's highest potential level in either subject will be thwarted, since one is not functioning in one's mother tongue, is a criticism that has been made by parents, especially those of pupils aspiring to study either subject further at university.

THE EUROPEAN BACCALAUREATE

The European Baccalaureate is the major goal of education in the European Schools. It has traditionally dominated the curriculum throughout secondary school and, some critics say, cast its shadow even as far as the primary school, by reason of the fact that pupils who are considered unlikely to pass it are said to be refused promotion from class to class or are 'counselled out' before they can reach it. At any rate, success rates in the region of 90 per cent of candidates are achieved in the Baccalaureate

Curriculum and Assessment: Eliding Foreignness

each year. They averaged 93 per cent from 1985 to 1989, and stood at 96.3 per cent in 1993. However, this was with an incidence of casualties along the way that has disturbed many parents and led to repeated criticisms of 'elitism', as we have seen. But the danger of excessively generous marking or 'grade inflation', especially in oral examinations where marks are invariably higher, has also been raised in a recent report (Hart 1994).

The attainment requirements for the final Baccalaureate examination are harmonised across the various language sections, so that in Mathematics, Natural Sciences, Philosophy and Latin the written examinations are identical, as well as in History and Geography – although taught through the three vehicular languages, while in the other subjects, including the languages themselves, comparable skills are required. The final examination consists of five written and four oral tests; the compulsory vehicular L2 has one written and one oral test, and subjects taught through this medium are examined almost according to the same criteria as those used for that language as if it were the mother tongue. In its structure therefore, which demands a compulsory core of subjects, as well as in its breadth, the European Baccalaureate is more akin to the typical continental school-leaving examination, and to the Scottish and Irish school-leaving examinations, than for instance to the General Certificate of Education (GCE) in England, Wales and Northern Ireland, or to the International Baccalaureate. The implications of the last point for future studies are discussed below.

The Baccalaureate is administered under the close supervision of an external examining board, appointed annually by the Board of Governors. This board consists of representatives of each of the Member States, who must satisfy the conditions governing the appointment of similar boards in their own countries. The chairman of the board will usually be a university professor, while the inspectors of the European Schools are also central to the process. Each written paper is evaluated by the pupil's class teacher, and again by a board member, the final mark being the arithmetical mean of the two. The written examination papers do not bear the candidate's name. For the oral examinations, the class teacher is also assisted by an external examiner.

In order to qualify for the Baccalaureate award, a pupil must undergo examination in each of the subjects studied during the sixth and seventh years. To pass the examination, a pupil must obtain an average of 60 per cent in all subjects, though she can pass with a mark as low as 30 per cent in some subjects.[1]

The structure of the examination, with corresponding weightings, is as follows:

1. Written examination in five subjects, viz. mother tongue, second language, two optional subjects and either Mathematics or a third option: 36%.
2. Oral examination in four subjects, viz. mother tongue and second language, History or Geography and an optional subject: 24%.
3. Internal assessment of all the subjects studied in the 7th year, including Religion/Ethics and Physical Education by means of:
   (a) internal school examinations   25%
   (b) continuous assessment   15%

It is important to note, therefore, that the teacher's assessment of the year's work in each subject of the 7th year, oral examination in four subjects and written examinations in five subjects, all contribute to the final result. The very searching nature of this examination needs to be fully communicated to any authority likely to be evaluating a pupil's Baccalaureate for admission to further studies. A candidate's weaker subjects, as well as the stronger ones, are taken into account – something which may not be done in evaluating the English students' A-levels in the GCE. Indeed, it is widely believed in the Schools that institutions which are unfamiliar with the European Baccalaureate may have tended to demand an unfairly high mark for admission.

Some individual comments made to the writer claimed that aspects of its organisation are inadequate, that standards in History and Geography are lower than in the Member States – thus constituting an insufficient base for the further study of these subjects, although this would scarcely be true of subjects taken at

Advanced Level. It is also felt that four hours for each written examination is too long. A maximum duration of three hours for any one examination paper seems more desirable, unless it can be demonstrated that the fourth hour adds significantly to the quality of answering observed in three, aside from the differential effects of fatigue on different candidates.

Besides being extended to include the languages of new Member States on occasion, the complex operation of the Baccalaureate has itself been revised by the Board of Inspectors. However the final comment here goes to Professor Asa Briggs: 'The European Baccalaureate ... has established itself in practice as one of the most imaginative ventures of recent years' (Briggs 1988).

Recognition of the European Baccalaureate

Article 5 of the Statute provides that the European Baccalaureate be fully recognised throughout the territory of the contracting countries as equivalent to the local school-leaving certificate, for the purpose of admission to universities and similar institutions of higher learning. This is legally subscribed to by each of the contracting parties. Nevertheless, such institutions frequently enjoy a measure of autonomy, and some problems have been reported. Besides, admission is not always guaranteed automatically to all holders of the local school-leaving certificate in some Member States, since more than the minimum requirement may be required by individual institutions.

The following evidence was assembled on how the holders of the Baccalaureate fared on leaving a European School:

1. A follow-up study of past pupils of the Varese School (unpublished).
2. An attempted comparability study by the Department of Education and Science in London (Department of Education and Science 1985).
3. A follow-up study by the writer of all those past pupils who had attended any constituent college of the National University of Ireland (unpublished).

A Singular Pluralism

    4. A further and more recent study published by the Department for Education in London (Department for Education 1994).

The first of these was carried out by means of a questionnaire sent by the Parents' Association of the European School in Varese to 86 alumni, of whom 46 (54 per cent) replied. Of the 21 who had studied in the Italian language section there, 19 were placed in some of the most distinguished universities in northern Italy, one in the Scuola Normale Superiore, and two in vocational training. No difficulties were reported. Fifteen past pupils of the German-language section were similarly placed in universities in Germany, Austria, Switzerland and England, as were seven pupils from the Dutch-language section. However, one past pupil of the French-language section complained of having to sit an examination in France which pupils from French lycées did not have to do, while another experienced problems in a UK university.

The Department for Education and Science in London pointed out that, although the number of subjects studied resulted in less specialisation than in A-levels, nevertheless this should be weighed against the breadth of the Baccalaureate. They concluded, on the basis of data collected from British universities, that while 'it is not possible to establish equivalence between the marks attained in the European Baccalaureate and A-level grades, [nevertheless] it is the experience of the European Schools that their pupils have normally acquitted themselves well on entering a British university, whatever the discipline followed …'.

The third study concerned the progress of nineteen past pupils of four European Schools, all of whom had been accepted as matriculated students into colleges of the National University of Ireland. No problem of admission had been encountered once all queries were fully answered, while the admissions officers seemed to be well informed regarding the Baccalaureate. Eleven of these alumni were still studying at the time of enquiry. Five had graduated, three with honours, two of them at a very high level. Three of the nineteen had retired from their courses.

The fourth study, based on data collected by Mr J. Foulkes of the School in Luxembourg, followed up all (n=111) former European Baccalaureate holders of 1989 who had entered higher education institutions in the United Kingdom. An analysis of the final degree results of those 86 who had graduated by 1993 showed that 86 per cent of them were awarded their degree with either first- or second-class honours, a very creditable performance indeed (Department for Education 1994). The conclusion of the DFE in the same source was that 'the degree results of EB holders [in UK universities] follow the national distribution of degree results by degree class. Drop-out rates are similar too' (p. 14).

A further unpublished study of past pupils of Culham found that 32 out of 40 were admitted to universities from Finland to Sicily, while a comment in a small number of the studies quoted above referred to having received inadequate general ('cultural') education in the European Schools attended (L. Blomme *et al.* 1989).

The indications are therefore that the European Baccalaureate has earned itself a high reputation in universities throughout Europe and that, on the whole, its holders are academically successful.

CONCLUDING COMMENTS ON THE CURRICULUM

'The curriculum of the European Schools has been criticised as being a pragmatic hotch-potch; philosophy, for example, is alleged to have been included because the French so wished. English critics, especially the proponents of "specialisation", have declared it to be unwieldy, comprising too many subjects and lacking in depth.' (Halls 1974).

The above comment by W.D. Halls, the eminent educationalist, gives a British view of the curriculum as it was in the 1970s. Unfortunately this comment ignores the balance, as well as the breadth, inherent in it, while its reaction to the presence of philosophy is altogether too insular, although the Blomme *et al.* study in Bergen may provide some evidence in support of the lack-of-depth comment, with reference to History for instance.

Three matters for final comment here are the language policy, the 'Europeanising effect', and the European dimension of the curriculum.

The Language Policy of the Schools

Bulwer (1992), by skilful use of 'naturalistic enquiry' in one of the European Schools, investigated the question 'In what way is bilingual education effective?' in the context of the teaching of History in L2. Since the pupils are using the L2 in a 'real communicative situation', Bulwer holds that 'their passive understanding will improve and gradually their use of language will become more confident'; he claims that the evidence adduced by him supports this.

Baetens Beardsmore and Kohls (1988) on the other hand, while painting a rather favourable picture of the Schools' curriculum, carried out a comparative study of 13-year-old Canadians (n=46) who had received 4,500 contact hours in an immersion programme of L2, and 13-year-old European School pupils (n=108) after receiving 1,300 classroom contact hours in an L2. The standard of achievement in both cases was highly comparable and this could be accounted for only 'in terms of the different background variables'. A similar study of 14-year-olds showed similarly comparable or better achievement levels of European School pupils (n=102) after 1,300 contact hours with L2 French, as against 4,500 contact hours for their Canadian counterparts (n=80). The authors' explanation is that the 'immediate pertinence' of L2 experience by the Europeans (who had to use their L2 in out-of-class and out-of-school peer group interaction), as against its perceived pertinence for the Canadian pupils (who did not use it outside language class), accounts for the former's superiority. Bulwer concludes that the *langue véhiculaire* is advantageous for the European School pupils in second language acquisition, though possibly at some cost to the content of the subject studied (History, in this case).

Tosi (1991), contrasting the multilingual (equal status) context and approach of the European School with the monolingual milieu of the International Baccalaureate schools and the 'diversity of equals' that characterises the former with the tendency towards 'assimilation' in the latter, concludes that 'the time spent on the second academic language does not cause the first ... to deteriorate'. The reward, he holds, 'is a population of educated bilinguals equally at ease with two languages, their own national culture, and the supranational European identity'. Apart from Bulwer's evidence of some loss 'with regard to national historical traditions and the study of history itself', one would agree with Tosi's summing up and with his view that the high cost of this 'privileged European education' has been an obstacle to the spread of this model elsewhere.

Finally what of the 'European dimension' itself in the European Schools? The concept originated with the Council of Europe in 1949 but, in the view of one critic, that body has been rather sensitive to fears of creating Eurocentric attitudes and has not produced a very coherent policy on this matter (Mickel 1986). EC Ministers for Education and the European Parliament have put forward proposals from time to time with particular reference to the need to develop a European identity through the cultivation of a European dimension in the schools; while there has been a considerable responsiveness at the level of individual schools and groups of schools in several places, progress is slow. One interesting review of this was carried out by Hart (1992), himself a former headmaster of a European School, in which an outline of progress in the European Schools is included.

Briefly, as Hart points out, the European dimension here 'lies in the daily fact of working, playing and living together, as much as in a deliberately European curriculum' (Hart 1992), while he goes on to outline the structures of school and syllabus that underpin their Europeanness, from the *langue véhiculaire* to the Model European Community Programme. One could specify many other exercises, e.g. the marvellously varied European Culture days based in Culham, which together support the conclusion that the spirit of Europe permeates the very air they breathe!

A joint conference of the EC Commission and the Council of

Europe's Council for Cultural Co-operation, held at Namur in 1990, while maintaining that our schools generally were not yet prepared for a Europe without frontiers, identified the European Schools in particular as having the potential to share valuable experience in the creation of separate language sections and in general for the intensive study of a foreign language.

The assessment study of the Bergen School (Blomme *et al.* 1989) found that 71.3 per cent of the 101 respondent pupils, felt that it was 'genuinely European'. Such feelings were on the whole endorsed by the respondents to the present writer's questionnaire of 1991. Teachers' representatives specified the Schools' 'European spirit'; pupil representatives praised the tolerance towards other nationalities experienced, while the parents who were questioned identified the 'truly European and unprejudiced attitudes of the pupils'. In short, it was a ringing endorsement for the Schools' treatment of the European dimension of education.

Chapter 3

THE HISTORY, GOVERNANCE AND MULTINATIONAL ACCOUNTABILITY OF THE EUROPEAN SCHOOLS

Something quite new in the history of educational institutions ...
Vernon Mallinson

INTRODUCTION

After about forty years' existence, the nine European Schools enrolled about 15,000 pupils as of August 1994. They are official educational establishments legally controlled by the governments of Belgium, Denmark, France, Germany, Greece, Ireland, Italy, Luxembourg, the Netherlands, Portugal, Spain and the United Kingdom,[1] as well as Austria, Finland and Sweden, in all of which they are regarded as public institutions. This chapter describes the system as a whole, beginning with a brief outline of its historical development. It goes on to describe the mode of governance and funding, the structure of authority and consultation. It also identifies and comments further on some of the Schools' unique features.

Historical Development

The kindergarten section of the first European School, that in Luxembourg, was opened at Easter 1953 on the initiative of parents of six nationalities, who were mainly employees of the European Coal and Steel Community, and especially that of the first Registrar of the Court of Justice of the European Communities, Mr Albert van Houtte, who was later to become the first Representative of the Board of Governors. In October of that year, a five-year primary section was added, bringing the total enrolment to 72 pupils.

This led the parents to request the High Authority to extend the experiment to the secondary level. The High Authority in turn invited each of the member governments' Departments of Education to contribute from its own culture and resources, and to second teachers from its own national system towards building up a new type of secondary school, based, as the primary school already was, on the languages and principles of education of the six Member States. As a result of an intergovernmental agreement, the first two secondary classes were opened in 1954, and continued growth thereafter saw that first school reach its full complement of grades in 1958. Meanwhile an agreement was concluded in July 1957 and was ratified by the Parliaments of the then six Member States, which made the European School an official intergovernmental institution.

In 1958 also the European Economic Community and the European Atomic Energy Community (EAEC) were established. This prompted the setting up of the first of the two European Schools to be built in Brussels, that in Uccle. In 1960 a further School was established in Varese for the children of the staff of the EAEC research centre in Ispra (Italy) between Lakes Maggiore and Como, and another at Mol in northern Belgium for the children of the staff of the EAEC Research Centre in Geel. Yet another School followed, in Bergen, near Amsterdam, for the children of the staff of the Joint Research Centre at Petten in 1963. The School in Karlsruhe was established in the same year. Brussels got its second European School (Woluwe) in 1976, a further school was established in Munich (Germany) in 1977 for the children of the staff of the European Patent Office, and finally one was set up in Culham (England) for the children of the staff of the JET (Joint European Thorus) project in 1978 (see Table 3.1). Thus was created, from a felicitous convergence of pragmatism and vision, the first intergovernmental school system and a new and important type of cultural convention, in order to guarantee schooling for the children of officials of the European institutions.

Table 3.1   Location and Date of Establishment of Each European School

Location	Date
Luxembourg	1953
Brussels I (Uccle)	1958
Mol (Belgium)	1960
Varese (Italy)	1960
Karlsruhe (Germany)	1963
Bergen (Holland)	1963
Brussels II (Woluwe)	1976
Munich (Germany)	1977
Culham (England)	1978
Brussels III (planned)	1997

The fact that they were established as an intergovernmental institution was of historical significance, both legally and culturally. The European Economic Community did not yet exist, while there was nothing in the European Coal and Steel Community's Treaty to sanction an educational initiative of this kind; hence the decision to share the costs between this Community, later the Communities, and the Member States.

Culturally and educationally, there were certain features of this hybrid system of schools that were far-sighted for their time. Possibly the structure of each School, with its combination of national and language groupings and European features, is the most obvious one. Other elements are the idea of an 'observation period' (at the Junior Secondary stage), the creation of a unified syllabus which, in the words of Van Houtte, 'if not a synthesis was at least a valid compromise' (Van Houtte 1984) between the different national systems. The decision to use *langues véhiculaires* would also be unusual, though the inclusion of Philosophy as a subject, and neutrality of teaching in the matter of freedom of conscience, would have been less so in the context of the time and place. Although some of these were already in evidence in varying degrees in some national systems, their combination, which resulted from very difficult negotiations, was to make an immensely challenging task at least achievable and to give these schools the unique character they still have today. The role on the Board of Governors accorded to both parents and teachers, and lastly the creation of the European Baccalaureate, must also be included here as courageous and inspired moves, adding to a structure which, for all the vicissitudes and criticisms encountered, has so far stood the test of time.

A tenth school has been sought since 1978, but it took until 1992 for this, the third Brussels School, to be decided upon; it will open its doors in 1997. Although requests have been made in the past to establish further European Schools elsewhere, these have not been acceded to, because the general policy of the Board of Governors is to create new schools only at the request of institutions of the European Community, or those in which it has a special interest.

The wide geographical spread of the Schools' locations is a feature which has the advantage of emphasising their supranational status and structure. It does, however, stretch their internal communications network, and adds considerably to their cost.

LEGAL BASIS AND FUNDING

The European Schools are unusual in that they are not a Community institution as such, but an intergovernmental body on which the Community is represented. They operated initially on the basis of the Statute of the European School which was signed in 1957. It was supplemented by a Protocol of 1962 which was ratified by the six founder members of the European Coal and Steel Community, and subsequently by the remaining six new Member States as they joined the EC.

In December 1992 the Ministers for Education agreed a new Statute for the European Schools and, as we have seen, this was signed in June 1994 and forwarded for ratification to each of the Member States. It seems likely that a number of innovations ushered in by the new Statute, especially the change from requiring unanimity to accepting a two-thirds majority vote (on most issues), will effectively improve the process of decision-making by the Board of Governors.

Other fundamental documents which govern the organisation and operation of the Schools are the following:

- the Collection of Decisions taken by the Board of Governors, which is published three times per year, i.e. following each meeting of that Board, in *Schola Europaea*, the pedagogical journal for all the Schools
- the General Rules of the European Schools
- the Statute of the Staff of the European Schools
- the Regulations of the European Baccalaureate
- the Syllabus, which has been approved by the Board of Governors for each class in every subject and is reviewed from time to time.

The Schools are largely financed (excluding premises) by the European Communities, which in 1990 provided 68 per cent of their budget, the importance of the principle of subsidiarity notwithstanding. This is done by means of an annual balancing subsidy (ECU89mn in 1993) which is entered in the Commission's budget. The remainder of the Schools' funding is provided by the Member States in the form of the payment of the national salaries of seconded teachers (about 22 per cent of the budget), a subsidy from the European Patent Office (5-6 per cent) and various other resources, including the school fees from 'non-entitled' pupils. It should be added that the Member States support the Schools in a variety of other ways, e.g. through the work of their inspectors, their counselling experts or school psychologists, in-service training of teachers, and providing free transport in some locations. The school buildings are made available free of charge by the host Member State, a matter that was described as 'disadvantageous' in the Motion for a Resolution by the Committee on Budgetary Control of the European Parliament in 1986 (European Parliament 1986a). Their reason was that it tended to slow down expansion of the schools when the need arose. There is some substance in this criticism, and in the view that the host governments do not always seem to be as responsive as they might be to requests for essential maintenance work to be done on the Schools within their territory.

Organisational Structure and Governance of the European Schools

The organs common to all the Schools, as established in the 1994 Statute, are the Board of Governors, the Secretary-General, the Board of Inspectors, and the Complaints Board. Each School is administered by its Administrative Board, and managed by the Head Teacher or Director with the help of the Assistant Directors. The Board of Governors or Conseil Supérieur is the supreme decision-making body of the European Schools' system. The relationship of this Board to its subordinate, advisory and related institutions and the framework of interrelated bodies at school level, are all illustrated in Figure 2. Legally this Board is a Council of Ministers in the same sense as the Council of Ministers of the Union. It comprises the Ministers for Education and/or Cultural Relations of the Member States, who in practice are usually represented by senior officials from their Ministries, as well as a member of the Commission of the European Communities, a representative designated by the Staff Committee and a representative of the Parents' Association. The right of the last two to vote is restricted to decisions on educational matters, while a pupils' representative may also be invited to attend relevant discussions.

The Board of Governors enjoys great autonomy, and has authority over all educational, administrative and financial matters.

History, Governance and Multinational Accountability

Figure 2   Organisational Structure of the European Schools: the Schools, the Board of Governors and the Parents

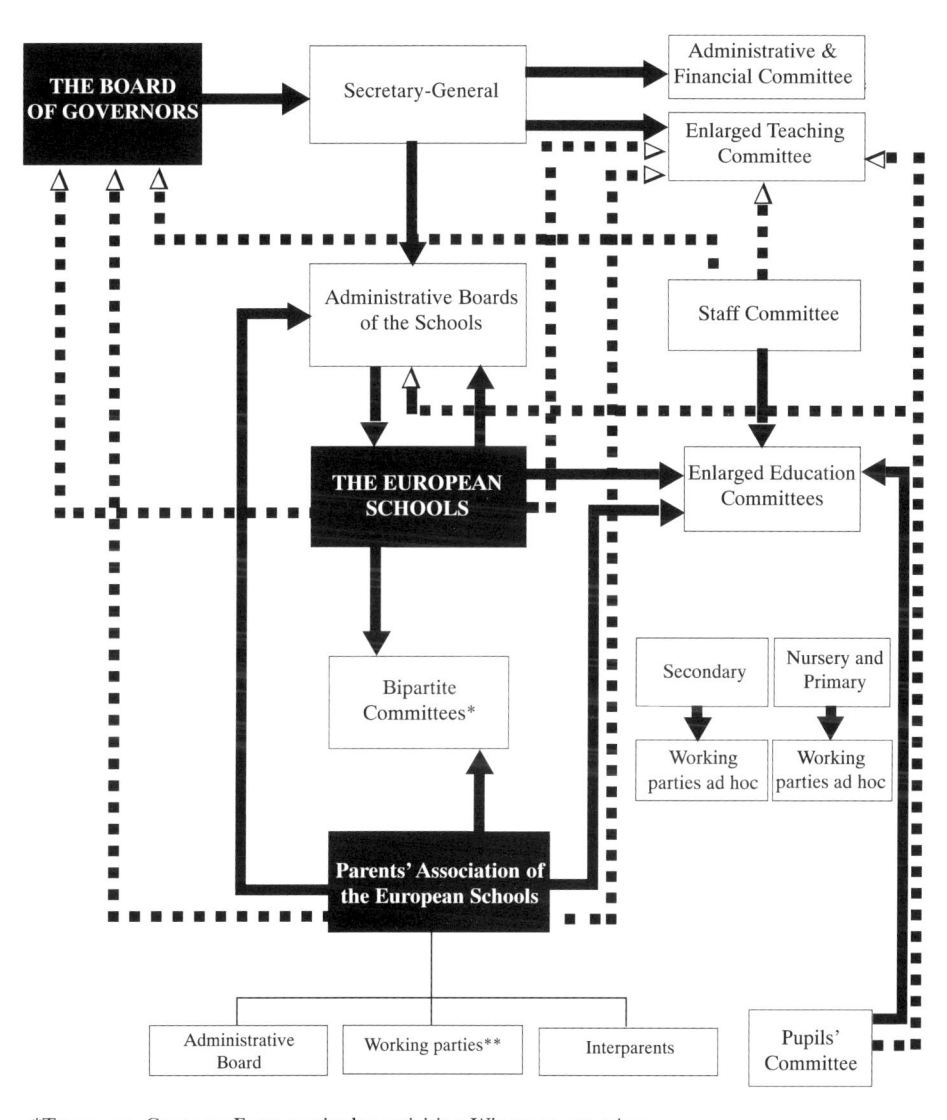

*Transport; Canteen; Extracurricular activities; Winter sports trips
**Educational matters; Information; Vocational guidance; Sale of second-hand books; Sport; Safety-Health

Participation without voting rights ■ ■ ■ ■▷
Participation with voting rights ━━━▶

A Singular Pluralism

Nevertheless, in 1986 the Committee of the European Parliament on Budgetary Control, in its Draft Report, took the view 'that, in order to stress the Community nature of the European Schools, the Board of Governors should have greater independence *vis-à-vis* the national authorities, and should use it in the interests of the Community' (European Parliament 1986b), whereas in 1993 the Board was described by one Parliament official as 'an uncontrollable institution'.

The following are accorded consultative status with the Board of Governors:

- for each school: the Director, two teachers, two parents
- the representatives of the associated institutions, e.g. Eurocontrol.

The Board of Governors must meet at least once a year.

Apart from the Board of Governors, the network of authority, representation and related activity, as illustrated in Figure 2, is the following:

The Secretary-General and the Deputy Secretary-General (formerly the Representative and Deputy Representative of the Board)

These are currently Mr J. Olsen and his deputy Mr G. Pinck, both full-time officials. They are based in the Central Office in Brussels.

Apart from directing the Secretariat, according to Article 14 of the Statute, the Secretary-General shall:

(a) be responsible to the Board of Governors
(b) represent the Schools in law
(c) act as Chairman of the Administrative Board of each School, which shall meet three times yearly.

The Administrative and Finance Committee (CAF)

A group of experts from each of the governments, composed in the same way as the Finance Committee of the European Communities' Council of Ministers. They are charged with studying all financial questions for the Board of Governors and meet five or six times each year.

The Enlarged Teaching Committee (Primary and Secondary)
This committee studies all educational questions to be submitted to the Board of Governors. Its composition is as follows:

- two Schools' inspectors from each Member State (one primary and one secondary)
- the Secretary-General and his deputy
- all the School Heads
- two representatives of the teaching staff (designated by all of them).
- two parents (designated by all the parents).

The Teaching Committee meets at least twice a year.

Board of Inspectors
Composed of inspectors appointed by the national education authorities, one primary and one secondary from each State, they carry out formal visits to the Schools from time to time, observe classes, issue directives, provide information on standards to Heads and teaching staff, and make proposals to the Board of Governors. They fulfil both a national and a European mission, but sometimes seem to find it difficult to convince their national authorities that their role in the European Schools is much wider than that of servicing a particular language section or pupils of their own nationality, e.g. each inspector is also given responsibility for curriculum development in a particular aspect of curriculum. Often carrying an unduly heavy workload, they fulfil, under difficult conditions, a role that is highly valued in the Schools; this view is based on submissions received by the writer in 1984 and again in 1991, and from personal attendance at Inspectors' and parents' meetings.

Interparents
Informal meetings of delegates of all Parents' Associations of the European Schools, held at regular intervals, which serve to co-ordinate common activities, to keep informed the parents' representatives in the various committees, and to

prepare joint proposals in writing for submission to the Board of Governors.

Teachers' Representatives

These are nominated by the various Schools' staff committees.
While the day-to-day affairs of each individual School are in the hands of the Director and his two deputies, there is also an Administrative Board in the School.

The Administrative Board of each European School

This comprises:

- The Secretary-General as Chairman
- Representative of the Commission of the European Communities
- Director of the School
- Two Deputy Directors ⎫ as advisers
- Administrator ⎭
- Two staff representatives
- Two parents' representatives
- Two pupils as observers, for matters of interest to them
- Representatives of organisations which have made an agreement with the Board for admission of more than 25 pupils.

The Administrative Board's main objective is to create a favourable atmosphere and suitable physical conditions for the proper functioning of the School. Meetings are held three times yearly. This Board is the decision-taking body at school level, and it prepares the proposal for the School's annual budget.

Director or Head of the European School

The Director or Head of each School is appointed by the Board of Governors for a term ranging from seven to nine years. When a new Head is appointed, he is usually of a different nationality from his predecessor. The Head of a European School is called upon to display leadership and linguistic, as well as social and administrative skills, of a high order. A broad measure of educational vision and pedagogical insight are also needed in this exacting role. In the past, all those appointed as School Directors had been male, but this situation changed in September 1994 when the first female Heads began work in Culham and Luxembourg.

The Deputy Head

Each Head has two Deputies – one for the nursery and primary, and one for the secondary section. Each one could be seen, under the Head's authority, as the leader of a unique team of teachers linking across the different language sections on a day-to-day basis, leading and facilitating curricular reforms and mediating the complex world of the European School to new teachers, as well as pupils and parents. At once an interpreter of policy and a motivator of teachers, his/her role is crucial to the welfare and progress of the School.

Education Council, Primary School
– Composition

- Head of School
- Deputy Head
- Four staff representatives
- Four parents' representatives.

Education Council, Secondary School
– Composition

- Head of School
- Deputy Head
- Three staff representatives
- Three students' representatives
- Three parents' representatives.

The above two committees meet regularly to discuss all matters concerning school life.

Side by side with structures of administration and responsibility, the flow of information and opportunities for communication make an important contribution to the life and effectiveness of a school community. In addition to the foregoing, each School has the staff group of each language section; working groups for Euromaths, Environmental Studies, second language teaching, European Hours, and for promotion from Kindergarten to Primary and from Primary to Secondary divisions; general staff meetings, and *ad hoc* committees to organise various events.

Parents' Association

The Parents' Association in each School enjoys official status by virtue of Article 24 of the Statute of the European Schools, specifically to:

– raise questions and proposals with the school administration, with respect to current affairs in the school
– organise extra-curricular activities in co-operation with the executive committee.

Although they could contribute indirectly to the deliberations of the Board of Governors, the Committee of Parents Associations (Interparents) had felt that their influence on policy-making at this level was less than it ought to be. It is significant therefore that, under the new Statute, their representative on the Board of Governors will now have the right to vote on educational issues. Besides this they can make an important contribution to the Enlarged Education Committees and at the level of the individual School, depending on the quality of their representatives at any given time.

At the level of the individual class, the parents may, and frequently do, appoint two class-parent representatives whose task is to act as a sensitive liaison between parents and teachers on matters of common concern. Other aspects of the parents' contribution to the life and working of the Schools are presented below.

Pupil Representatives

The pupils in each School appoint representatives to a Pupils'

Association; these in turn appoint delegates to a combined Pupils' Association (Comité Supérieur, abbreviated as Cosup) for all nine Schools. Their status to date remains consultative, and the procedure seems to work satisfactorily. Nevertheless they themselves are seeking a more formal recognition of their entitlement to participate in policy-making up to the highest level in the system.

It was particularly interesting to note that pupil representatives were invited to give evidence in person to the Special Hearing on the Schools of the European Parliament's Committee on Youth, Culture, Education, Information and Sport, in 1986, and to witness the high quality of their presentations to that hearing.

Internal School Management and Consultation

One notable feature of the internal organisation of the Schools is the absence of a departmental structure. This might be a matter of no great concern perhaps, under other conditions, at least in smaller and more homogeneous schools. But the 'Chinese boxes' structure of each European School is such that the usual divisions of any school are, as we have seen, multiplied greatly here. Hence the need for formally recognised heads of department, who will facilitate the individual teacher and foster teamwork among colleagues, as well as helping common pedagogical understanding and strategies to develop. However, progress has been made in recent years in creating some middle management structures, with the establishment of 'subject co-ordinators' in some, but not yet all, Schools. Their role is both pastoral and administrative/pedagogical. Their chief functions are to facilitate pupil transition into the School, to harmonise the demands made on pupils, as well as criteria and modes of assessment, and to ensure the more effective use of resources. This innovation received favourable comment, especially from parents' representatives, in the author's follow-up study of 1991.

The machinery of consultation between School authorities, parents and teachers, though slow, is on the whole good. However, both from submissions received and personal attendance at meetings of teachers and parents, the writer has found the parents of pupils divided on whether or not they were accorded a role in decision-making (or *Mitbestimmung* in the German system) greater than is usual at school level in the national education systems. In the European Schools where parents of very diverse national backgrounds and experience bring a wide range of sometimes conflicting expectations to bear on their children's schooling, it is to be expected that many issues, which would find unanimity in a national context, will become highly contentious here. Inevitably, therefore, the decisions reached will, in turn, leave some parents dissatisfied from time to time.

The Structure of Authority of the European Schools

The organisation and funding of public education in the Member States is normally carried out either at national level or at regional/local level, or based on some balance between them; indeed it is frequently the preserve of the national government, acting on behalf of the people, and with or without the help of private institutions. The superstructure of authority over the school in turn will commonly entail accountability at both the local and national levels, locally through a School Board and regionally or nationally through the agency of the schools' inspectorate, for instance, or through a further tier of government at regional and/or state level. Though still seen as an innovation (even an undesirable one) in some places, the need for School Boards is more or less universally accepted. Thus, while pointing out that their creation and functioning were bound to expose some conflict, Beare nevertheless holds that they 'have a political legitimacy which justifies their existences ... and it is safer to have them than not to have them' (Beare 1993).

In the case of the European Schools, there are two main levels of accountability, the local one operating at the level of the Administrative Board of the individual School, and the central one, with the Board of Governors and the inspectors acting, as it were, in place of national government. There is a further level of accountability here, however: this one to the European Commission with its representative on the Board of Governors; it also represents on the Board the interest of the European Parliament.

Some commentators hold the view that a clearer role for the European Parliament could further enhance democratic accountability at the European level, and make for the greater harmonisation of national policies and practices *vis-à-vis* the European Schools. This position has been repeatedly supported by the Commission, as was pointed out in the Memorandum on the Motion for a Resolution by Dr Peus (Commission of the EC 1986b). However, as emerged in the presentations to the Public Hearing of the Committee of the European Parliament in 1986 (cited above), there are others who feel it would be better for the Parliament not to become more closely involved with the Schools than it is at present, on the basis that maintaining a more distant but vigilant watching brief is its best role.

There remains, however, the danger that the Schools could be used from time to time as a pawn in the ongoing power struggle between the Council of Ministers, the Commission and the Parliament, a struggle which became more visible at the time of the Maastricht Treaty. Democratic accountability is of course essential, but political point-scoring could undermine educational progress in the European, no less than in the national, education arena.

Evaluating the Quality of Administration

The European Schools have been, and still remain, very much a single system, rather than a federation of autonomous or semi-autonomous units. In this, the totality resembles a national system, but one which is centrally rather than locally or individually administered, a feature that was already criticised in the Walkhoff report of 1975 (European Parliament 1986b). Described as being 'increasingly subject to political pressure' in one submission received by the writer, it is closer to a 'continental' model, e.g. that of France or Belgium, than is found in some other Member States, subject to change though many of these are at present. The resemblance is seen particularly in the breadth of decision-making which is reserved to the Board of Governors, rather than being devolved to school level, thus reflecting an initial choice historically of one of a number of possible concepts of the balance that should obtain between the central and local administration of schooling.

While no direct evidence emerged, in the present research, of serious tension between the School Directors and the Board of Governors, there were indications of a feeling among the Directors that their role is unduly circumscribed (European Schools 1988). It is disappointing to find this situation perpetuated in the new Statute, in which no special role in policy-making is accorded to them, nor is the individual School allowed any greater latitude in responding to local needs than was the case in the past.

This is also disappointing in view of recent trends emerging in several countries, following a worldwide debate on the administration of education systems. For instance, from a review of research in the USA, Australia, New Zealand and Britain, Caldwell concludes as follows: 'Research on school effectiveness and improvement … consistently support a relatively high degree of autonomy at school level … minimising the number of constraining rules and regulations', and while 'a strong central role is important [it] should be limited to establishing a vision for the systems as a whole, setting expectations and standards for student learning and providing strong support for Schools' (Caldwell 1993). What should be sought is neither centralisation nor decentralisation for its own sake, but whatever balance or combination of these is likely to be most efficient and effective in achieving the educational objectives of these Schools in view of their particular context and mission.

Yet the Director of a European School has a more narrowly defined range of powers than his or her counterpart in either a typical secondary school in the United Kingdom, in Ireland, or in many international schools in Europe. While it may be argued that the centralised structure arises 'naturally' from the degree of accountability required to satisfy the hierarchy of institutions to which they are responsible here, it is nevertheless possible to imagine a less rigid and less prescriptive system, which would be democratically accountable and pedagogically effective at the same time.

The further argument that common standards and a common curriculum are seen as vital in order to ensure the 'currency' value of the European Baccalaureate is a more convincing one, though the persistent variation in standards observed between the different language sections tends to weaken that argument in turn. Suffice it to say that the highly unified structure of the system as a whole is not necessarily the only one that might have been adopted, and that an inherent inflexibility of policies, which renders it difficult to take problems of individual schools into account, still needs to be recognised and overcome.

How effective, then, is the administration of this unified system? In the past, perhaps not as effective as its proponents might have assumed. Thus, in spite of the impressive superstructure of governance and administration, a considerable time-lag was observed between the promulgation of regulations by the Board of Governors and their implementation at the level of the individual School and classroom. For instance, in 1977 the Board of Governors decided that pupils in the primary sections should normally be promoted to a higher class each year, unless in exceptional cases. A similar decision with reference to promotion from 1st to 2nd, and from 2nd to 3rd year secondary, was reached in May 1980, while a similar new provision for promotions from 3rd to 4th and from 4th to 5th years was issued in May 1982. In the event, the incidence of non-promotion or repeating, which had been rising since 1978/79, continued to increase until 1982, beginning to show a downturn only in 1982/83.

A second instance refers to the long-standing demand for a Cycle Court or Intermediate examination of some sort for pupils who, for whatever reason, drop out of the secondary school at the end of their fifth year. Although an Intermediate evaluation was approved by the Board of Governors on 1 February 1989, to be implemented for the first time in 1991/92, it finally came into operation only in 1994.

Both incidents are taken as illustrating the point that in the European Schools' system, despite its tight structuring and highly uniform character, decisions of the high authority have taken a long time to result in action on the classroom floor. Whether this would happen today seems less likely because there now are systems in place to ensure that directives are carried out, although from time to time the Board of Governors takes decisions which remain neither speedily nor uniformly applied.

Some advantages and disadvantages of the centralised and unified system, and the consequent uniformity engendered throughout the Schools may be pointed out.

(a) *Possible Advantages:* Ease of administration, control and inspection; greater possibilities for collegial support among directors and teachers across the different Schools; enhanced cost-effectiveness; the underpinning of the international acceptability of the single Baccalaureate; the enhanced transparency of a publicly accountable system.

(b) *Possible Disadvantages:* A disinclination in the past to form links with and exploit very different national and local conditions for educational purposes; diminished innovativeness and responsiveness to change; almost total isolation of the Schools from the local systems; uniformity, which also could render impersonal what should be, first and foremost, very caring institutions.

Several of the foregoing administrative issues, both positive and negative, emerged in the submissions made to the writer in 1984 and again in 1991. These will be dealt with here as follows: first, those which had been redressed by administrative measures during the intervening period; second, features or policies of longer standing which were now favourably commented upon by respondents; and third, some of those that were still seen as major unsolved problems.

Two initiatives, both well received, were the extension of remedial teaching to the primary sections of all the Schools, allied to their extended capacity for the inclusive education of some disabled pupils, and the institution of a guidance centre in one secondary section – both measures still felt by some to be insufficient, however. Besides, the establishment of in-service courses for teachers, the structuring of a 'middle management' tier by way of subject co-ordinators, and the setting up of an Intermediate evaluation at the end of fifth year secondary – all are recent developments which were widely welcomed in the 1991 submissions. Such developments had been called for in the writer's 1984 report, but the number of initiatives undertaken by the Board of Governors since then is evidence that the system *is* responsive to widespread needs in the Schools as a whole, and deserves public credit for this. Indeed, in so far as certain of these innovations are relatively new, if not unknown, in some Member States, then the European Schools deserve all the greater credit for them, however long the innovations may be established in still other systems. It is still too early, however, to evaluate fully the adequacy of the innovations mentioned in meeting the needs that they were designed to overcome.

Second are those more long-standing features and policies which received favourable comment in the 1991 submissions. Prominent here were, first, the teaching of a second language from first-year primary and the general *langue véhiculaire* policy, and second, the reformed structure which has widened subject choice in the Baccalaureate. Both received a strong endorsement in 1991.

What then of educational *problems* which had been identified in 1984 and still remained unsolved in 1991. Among these, two major issues received the most frequent mention. They were (i) the 'comprehensive intake – academic output' phenomenon, i.e. the persisting high failure rates, attributed to the heavily academic orientation of the Schools; and (ii) the divergent approaches to teaching and examining, observed between the different language sections' teachers. Following these came: the perceived isolation of the Schools from local contact; the lack of suitable textbooks; overcrowding in four Schools; and inadequate teacher preparation – all still matters of concern to the respondents, despite their having received varying degrees of attention from the Board of Governors and others in authority.

In conclusion, distance is an ever-present problem in the

European Schools' system – physical distances between home and School for many pupils, between School and home country, between School and School. To these must be added the psychological distances between the different linguistic, cultural and pedagogical traditions represented. Although the structures for democratic consultation are favourably commented upon, the cumbersome superstructure, which may have been an inevitable result of such a hybrid institution, was also liable to create distances as well as overcome them. Nevertheless it has shown itself capable, however slowly, of initiating and implementing change on a number of urgent issues. The fact that its record on this criterion is probably at least as good as that of many national systems augurs quite well for the future.

Chapter 4

THE SCHOOL COMMUNITIES OF TEACHERS, PARENTS AND PUPILS

> The European Schools are fascinating, stimulating and superbly successful. Their advantages do outweigh their disadvantages. But there is much discontent.
>
> A Brussels parent

To the outside observer, undoubtedly the most striking feature of the teaching staff and pupils of a European School, and the pupils' parents, is their cosmopolitan, polyglot character, though to leave it at that would be superficial. The culture shock of a new teacher's first encounter with the living reality of these communities, as well as the complexities and rewards of sharing the daily life of such a school, have been well described in several of the contributions by teachers in various issues of *Schola Europaea*, the bulletin common to all the Schools (see, for example, Opitz 1990). In this chapter we look in turn at these three groups – the teachers, the parents and the pupils – which together comprise the community of the European Schools.

THE TEACHERS

Nearly a thousand teachers seconded from at least twelve cultural traditions, educated in and trained for as many national school systems, and speaking nine or more native languages among them – this is a thumbnail sketch of the combined teaching staffs of the European Schools to date. The mere encounter of cultures, one feels, cannot but be enriching for themselves and their pupils. While the potential for divergent views could be considerable, the potential for growth through diversity must distinguish these Schools as a rich cultural resource for the creation of a united Europe.

The schools, of course, do not all have an equal mixture of nationalities. As of 1994, the Luxembourg School was the only one to have teachers seconded from all twelve Member States; the two Brussels Schools came a close second, while even the smallest school, Mol, had teachers of no less than six nationalities. Table 4.1 illustrates the uniquely multinational composition of the combined teaching staffs of the Schools, and incidentally the extent to which the national governments contribute, by way of paying teachers' salaries, to the cost of the Schools.

The visitor can be exhilarated or bewildered by lively staff room conversations which move easily among three, four or more languages. While there were Dutch, Italian, French, Belgian, German and British teachers in all the Schools, there were teachers from Luxembourg and Ireland in seven Schools, from Spain in five, with Greece, Denmark, and Portugal represented only in a minority. Diversity and readily accepted cultural differences are the keynote, with a rich sharing of common professional experiences from distinct educational traditions.

Yet the pupils' awareness of the linguistic and national differences among the teachers seems to recede as they move up through the Schools, and to matter less to them in their interaction with teachers than, for instance, a 'generation gap', or one's quality as a teacher in the classroom. *Plus ça change, plus c'est la même chose!*

The European Schools

Celebrating

Learning

Playing

```
         COMMISSION
         DES COMMUNAUTES
         EUROPEENNES
```

Le Président

Les Ecoles européennes constituent une réalité étroitement unie à la construction européenne.

La création de la première école à Luxembourg en 1953, dont nous célébrons le 40ème anniversaire cette année, suivie par la création des autres écoles un peu plus tard, a été motivée par la nécessité d'assurer le bon fonctionnement des Institutions communautaires et l'accomplissement de leurs missions en permettant la présence sur les lieux de travail de fonctionnaires provenant de différents Etats membres avec leurs familles.

Cette vocation originelle serait déjà un motif suffisant pour rendre hommage aux Ecoles européennes. Mais la contribution de ces écoles à la construction européenne ne s'arrête pas là.

Les écoles, comme l'a déclaré le Parlement européen à plusieurs reprises, sont en effet devenues un laboratoire sociologique et pédagogique unique au monde et irremplaçable pour la création d'une structure scolaire européenne dans laquelle se poursuit tous les jours l'effort de promouvoir les valeurs communes tout en préservant la riche diversité culturelle et linguistique des Etats membres de la Communauté.

"Européiser sans dénationaliser" est la devise toujours fidèle à l'idée de Robert Schuman selon laquelle "l'Europe n'est pas la négation de la patrie".

Cet ambitieux et noble projet éducatif s'est développé dans le cadre d'une coopération intergouvernementale renforcée par une participation significative de la Communauté.

A letter of congratulations from Jacques Delors, President of the Commission of the European Union, in 1993 on the occasion of the fortieth anniversary of the founding of the Schools.

Cette architecture équilibrée a permis que les équipes de professionnels de l'éducation et de l'administration éducative qui se sont succédé se consacrent à l'exécution de ce projet en donnant le meilleur d'eux-mêmes.

Les fruits de leurs efforts sont là : enseignement commun conçu en fonction de programmes harmonisés qui permettent en même temps de donner à des enfants, originaires de différents Etats membres, une formation scolaire dans leur langue maternelle et surtout un apprentissage quotidien de l'autre. Garçons et filles de diverses langues et nationalités apprennent à se connaître, à s'estimer et à vivre ensemble dans la compréhension réciproque, le respect et la tolérance.

Il m'apparaît indispensable que toute cette richesse, dont les bénéficiaires immédiats sont les propres élèves des Ecoles européennes, soit exploitée de la meilleure façon possible par les systèmes éducatifs nationaux des différents Etats membres.

Savoir inculquer à la jeunesse les idéaux européens et surtout faire en sorte qu'ils se traduisent dans le vécu de tous les instants, est sans nul doute la voie la plus belle et la plus certaine vers une paix durable, seule garante de l'Europe, telle qu'on l'a beaucoup rêvée avant nous, et que nous avons la chance de construire.

Jacques DELORS

COMITÉ D'ACTION
POUR LES
ÉTATS-UNIS D'EUROPE

PASSY 52-36
KLÉBER 24-64

83, AVENUE FOCH, PARIS XVIᵉ

le 21 décembre 1962

Monsieur le Président,

    Je suis très heureux d'apprendre que vous comptez célébrer le dixième anniversaire de l'Ecole Européenne. Cette commémoration vient peu de temps après celle du Marché Commun du charbon et de l'acier et nous rappelle que l'Ecole Européenne est un élément important de la contribution que la CECA a faite, et fait encore, à la formation de l'Europe.

    Comme vous le savez, ma fille cadette, Marianne, a suivi les cours de 1953 à 1955 et j'ai pu, par ma propre expérience, constater l'influence d'une école qui n'est pas seulement européenne par sa composition, mais aussi par sa méthode d'enseignement et les perspectives qu'elle ouvre aux jeunes.

    Ce qui me semble particulièrement encourageant dans l'expérience que vous poursuivez, c'est le sens des réalités qui vous a amené à appliquer une méthode nouvelle. L'Ecole Européenne a commencé modestement comme l'école des fonctionnaires des institutions de la Communauté. Mais elle n'a jamais été une simple école dite " de diplomates" où les nationalités se juxtaposent, sans que les programmes soient fusionnés. Dès le début, vous y avez apporté un enseignement bilingue et une vue européenne des choses qui ont donné un caractère nouveau à votre entreprise. Enfin, en créant des diplômes valables dans tous les pays membres, vous avez rendu un service précieux à la jeunesse. C'est parce que vous avez créé des changements dans les faits que des réformes qui pouvaient peut-être de loin paraître modestes ont en fait eu un effet profond et commencent à s'étendre. Le succès des Ecoles Européennes montre qu'à l'avenir, l'Europe pourra avoir sa culture sans que les nations qui la composent perdent la leur.

    Permettez-moi de vous féliciter encore de vos efforts et de vous exprimer mes vœux les meilleurs pour la réussite continue de cette expérience de l'unification des Européens de demain.

votre cordialement

Jean Monnet

Monsieur Albert VAN HOUTTE
Représentant du Conseil Supérieur
de l'Ecole Européenne
Boulevard de la Foire
LUXEMBOURG (Grand Duché)

A letter of congratulations from Jean Monnet, a founding father of the European Communities, in 1962 on the occasion of the tenth anniversary of the founding of the Schools.

Luxembourg

Bruxelles I

Culham

Varese

Bruxelles 11

Bergen N.H.

Mol

Karlsruhe

München

Table 4.1   National Origins of Seconded Teachers (1994)*

Country of Origin	Number of Teachers
	n=
Belgium	142
Denmark	28
France	127
Germany	179
Greece	24
Ireland	30
Italy	105
Luxembourg	23
Netherlands	74
Portugal	25
Spain	39
United Kingdom	160
Total	956

*Based on data supplied by the Central Office, August 1994

Pedagogical Bulletin, Teacher Mobility and Secondment

A sense of this diverse richness may also be gleaned from *Schola Europaea,* the official bulletin which appears four or five times a year. Besides conveying official information from the meetings of the Board of Governors and the Boards of Inspectors, it also provides a forum for teachers to report on curriculum innovation, accounts of yearly events in the life of the Schools, e.g. school tours, theatrical productions, news of teachers' arrivals and departures, and so on. Articles ranging from the anecdotal to the scholarly, and written by the teachers themselves, add to its depth and colour, for where else will one encounter a school journal written in nine or ten languages – including two alphabets (Greek and Roman) – which nevertheless finds common ground, not only in the universal culture of schools, but also that of Europe? Such a widely scattered, somewhat isolated, network of Schools needs the written words of a bulletin like this to perform a catalytic role in creating mutual awareness of difficulties and in recording achievements or innovations. Great credit is due to those responsible for producing it from year to year. The individual Schools also publish 'school annuals' from year to year, whether produced by staff or pupils, which capture and convey the passing scene of school life and pupils' perennial wit.

Most of the teachers in the European Schools are seconded to them by the Education Ministry of the Member State in which they have been employed. The duration of teachers' secondment to the Schools has long been a controversial issue. It has now been fixed by the 1994 statute, under which it will not exceed nine years in the case of teachers who entered the system as of 1 September 1989.

Initially it was intended to be for a limited period so as to facilitate the dissemination of their European School experience among colleagues on their return (Van Houtte 1984). However, different national traditions existed; and a tendency seems to have developed for many to extend their secondment indefinitely and for some to move from one School to another within the system. This led the Walkhoff Report in 1975 and, some years later, the headmasters to call for a common system of teacher secondment. Again, the inspectors commented favourably on the 'growing tendency to limit the duration of secondment of teachers' and advocated that this practice become general(Inspectors 1984). Dr Peus, in the Working Document of 1986, found that differences in the duration of secondment were still a source of conflict among teachers, but that 'most Schools agree that secondment should last between nine and fifteen years' (European Parliament 1986). More recently, as we have seen, the Board of Governors established a working party to consider a request of the European Parliament regarding the uniform implementation of the rule requiring repatriation after nine years' secondment.

The seconded teachers will be fully qualified for and experienced in teaching at the relevant level in their own country. A lacuna may occur, however, in the case of those countries which do not have a pedagogical (as distinct from a 'scientific') training course requirement for teaching in their secondary or upper secondary schools, though these exceptional situations are also changing.

The fact that teachers from some Member States must resign from their teaching post at home in order to accept appointment in a European School, and without a guarantee of employment on completing their contract, is seen as a disincentive by prospective applicants from those countries. This may in turn limit the range of candidates available from these countries.

Indeed, some countries seem to experience difficulty from time to time in filling their quota of allocated posts. Thus in Culham in 1989/90 two vacancies existed for Italian teachers, neither of which was filled and, according to the School's annual report, neither would be filled. In the same year the United Kingdom authorities could not find a replacement for an appointed teacher. These situations, however, are very rare. In most cases teachers are appointed and present at the beginning of the school year.

A second category of teacher in the Schools, known as *chargé de cours*, is recruited locally and on a non-permanent basis, in order to supplement the work of the seconded teachers. In practice, nearly all of them will be qualified teachers.

The employment of a further group, known as *conseillers d'education*, is a concept peculiar to some but quite unfamiliar in many Member States. Their duties range from supervising pupils during recreation to registering daily attendance, following up absentees, and even teaching on occasion. The preparation of end-of-term reports to the parents is also their responsibility, whereas in many countries this is strictly the duty of the regular class teacher.

Teacher Selection and Employment

It is noteworthy that the head teacher of a European School is usually permitted little or no role in appointing seconded teachers to his/her own staff, this power being reserved by the national authorities. While this position would be unacceptable in certain Member States' school systems – and to executives in many business and professional organisations as well – it seems to be accepted practice in the schools of other States in the EU and in some countries' systems of 'schools abroad'. It too has been a bone of contention in the European Schools and was described as unsatisfactory by the School Directors both in 1984 and 1991.

In its Memorandum to the European Parliament in 1986 (European Parliament 1986a), the European Schools' Staff Committee made a number of cogent points, beginning with the observation that 'experience shows that an excellent national teacher is not necessarily a good European teacher' (p.4) and suggesting that extremely high levels of communicative, linguistic and pedagogical skill are 'in theory' demanded. They then went on to point out that since many states would regard any move to involve the Heads in teacher selection as 'an infringement of their sovereignty, it is up to the [Member States] to do their best to fill vacancies by applying their own criteria' (p.5). Now if criteria of excellence that apply in the national context may not, as they claim, be relevant in a European School, does it make sense that the Principal, who knows not only the system but the individual School intimately, should be excluded from selecting his or her own staff? The teachers' representatives, regrettably, did not base their case on considerations of the interest of the School or the pupil. They did however advocate 'a preparatory inservice training period in a national or European environment', which seems a very constructive idea and might even appear to be essential, though scarcely adequate, to counteract an unsuitable appointment on its own, should this occur. In fact the Peus Report to the European Parliament (1986) in its recommendations called clearly for 'school headmasters to be granted a greater say in the selection of teachers'. Some national authorities, however, have begun sending short-listed candidates on a short advance visit to the school in question, thus giving both sides an opportunity to reach a mature appraisal of the situation, and in some cases the Principal of the School participates in the final interviews of candidates for teaching posts in his or her School. Nevertheless, it remains a problem for which harmonisation between the national authorities is urgently needed since the existing procedure could militate against the best interests of the individual school and its staffing.

The following table gives the total number of seconded teachers in each of the European Schools, as of 1994.

Table 4.2   Teaching Staff in 1994*

School	Seconded Teachers
	n=
Luxembourg	184
Brussels I	210
Brussels II	141
Mol	59
Varese	87
Karlsruhe	81
Bergen	65
Munich	63
Culham	71
Total	961

*Data supplied by Central Office, 1994

With regard to the relative size of the Schools, while typical school size varies widely from country to country, none of the European Schools would be regarded as small in certain parts of the EU. Their size, together with the overcrowded conditions in some of them, added to their cultural complexity and unusual mission, indicates just how crucial is the choice of person for the post of Director.

Teacher and Task in the European Schools

Any school system is as good as its teachers, or rather as good as the match between teacher and task. The European Schools are fortunate in attracting many talented and versatile teachers, who will already have had a proven record of professional achievement on their home ground, and who have contributed to the distinguished reputation which this system now enjoys.

But the demands of teaching in a European School are unique

in many ways. Apart from the fact that the newly appointed teacher and his or her family are frequently expatriate for the first time, she/he is expected now to teach a somewhat different pupil population within a new administrative and curricular framework. Certain contextual assumptions, which were shared without question at home, may now be open to question or prove to be irrelevant here. The teacher's role is always influenced by the expectations of others – pupils, colleagues and parents in particular. But pupil behaviour encountered in the multicultural climate of a European School may be new and trivial, or new and challenging. The pupil who insists on doing her knitting throughout a language class, for instance, may be overlooked in one culture, but considered grossly insubordinate in another. Again, a class may be taught the first lesson of the day by a teacher who introduces himself by his first name, addresses the pupils by theirs, and maintains an informal rapport throughout. In the next lesson the same pupils may be taught by another teacher who is to be addressed as Mr X or Doctor Y, and whose manner, deriving from a different national tradition, is entirely formal and impersonal. The impact of such contrasting teaching styles on the pupils could reciprocally provide a mild culture shock for the teacher.

Even the teacher's attitude to aspects of the subject-matter taught may undergo radical reappraisal on moving to a European School; for instance, the history teacher's lesson on the Battle of Waterloo, which was acceptable to his pupils at home in England, may not go unchallenged by his class of French pupils in a European School, while perhaps the German or Spanish history teacher's knowledge of Ireland's or Denmark's contribution to European democracy could well be far less than that of the Irish or Danish pupil whom he is teaching.

More problematic still, however, may be the implications for pupils of the divergent notions which teachers of different nationalities can hold as to what constitutes a 'pass' or 'fail' mark in an examination (as we have seen in Chapter 2).

The teacher in a European School must constantly cope with the reality that most of the pupils are also expatriates, to whom at times the language of the classroom will be a foreign language, but who look to him to respect, protect and nurture their own developing cultural identity. When he is the sole representative of that culture in the pupil's life for five or six hours a day and far removed from its living reality, this teacher, especially in the primary section, is indeed in an exposed position. Besides having a considerable commitment both to his own national culture and to Europe, the successful teacher in a European School will need to be adaptable and, even in some instances, capable of teaching in two languages, at least one of them a *langue véhiculaire* of the School. Capability to teach more than a single subject specialisation is also important, while some talent in music, art, crafts, or sport is a useful bonus.

How well matched then is the teacher to the task in the European Schools? In the writer's study of 1984, a number of problems emerged as those most frequently identified, not only by the parents, directors and pupils, but also in most cases by the teachers themselves. Some major ones were:

1. The teachers are inadequately prepared for, and have problems in adapting to, a European School.
2. They have different national styles of teaching.
3. The Schools are isolated from pedagogic innovation.
4. Some teachers know their subject but cannot teach it.
5. Teachers may lose touch with their home system.
6. Many teachers are not qualified to teach their mother tongue as a *foreign language*, but are now required to do so.
7. Teachers rely too much on teaching facts rather than teaching pupils how to think analytically.
8. 'French teachers' style is too teacher-centred'.
9. There is a 'generation gap' between older teachers and pupils.
10. Some teachers remain too long in the European School.

Clearly some of these comments might be heard of any sample of teachers anywhere, while others seem to derive from the particular character of these Schools.

It should be pointed out that a growing body of research is

A Singular Pluralism

now showing that, for a variety of reasons – and they vary from one context to another, teaching is seen as an increasingly demanding occupation in many school systems; there is even evidence of a certain amount of stress and 'burnout', especially related to working conditions, among a number of teachers in many places.

One scheme for conceptualising in the abstract the suitability of the teacher to the task, is given in Figure 3.

Figure 3 Teacher-Task Match

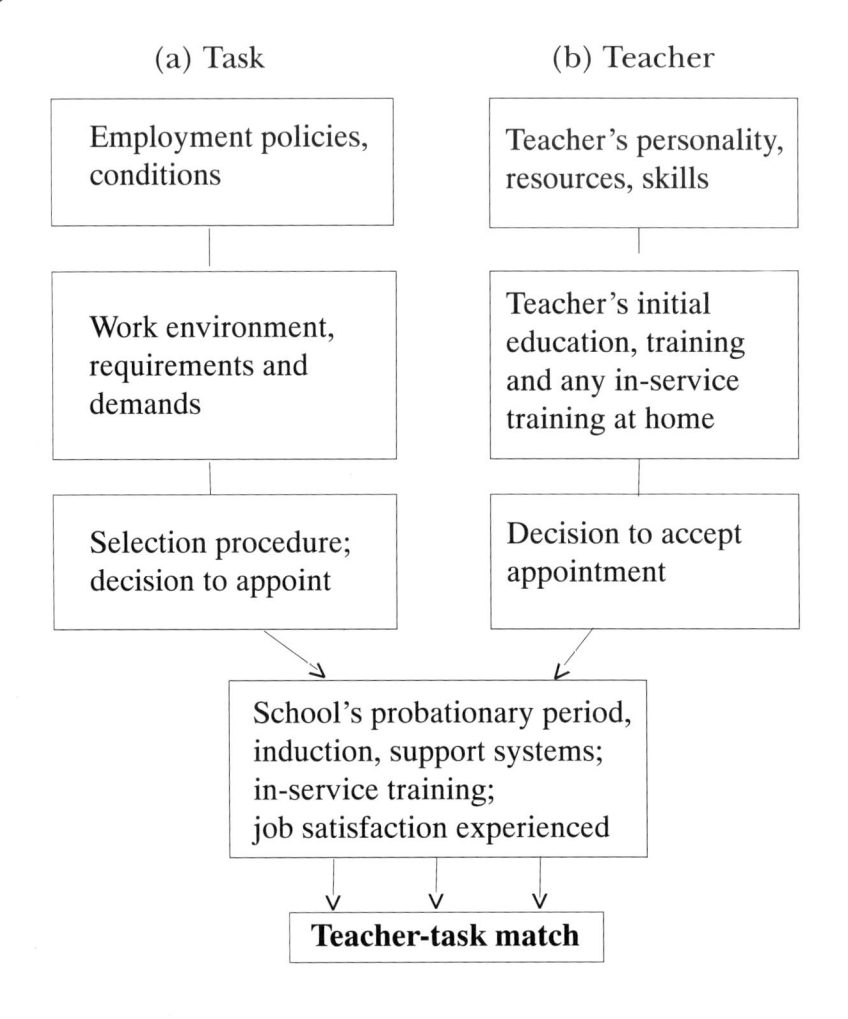

```
        (a) Task                           (b) Teacher

┌─────────────────────────┐       ┌─────────────────────────┐
│ Employment policies,    │       │ Teacher's personality,  │
│ conditions              │       │ resources, skills       │
└─────────────────────────┘       └─────────────────────────┘
            │                                 │
┌─────────────────────────┐       ┌─────────────────────────┐
│ Work environment,       │       │ Teacher's initial       │
│ requirements and        │       │ education, training     │
│ demands                 │       │ and any in-service      │
│                         │       │ training at home        │
└─────────────────────────┘       └─────────────────────────┘
            │                                 │
┌─────────────────────────┐       ┌─────────────────────────┐
│ Selection procedure;    │       │ Decision to accept      │
│ decision to appoint     │       │ appointment             │
└─────────────────────────┘       └─────────────────────────┘
               ↘                       ↙
       ┌────────────────────────────────────────┐
       │ School's probationary period,          │
       │ induction, support systems;            │
       │ in-service training;                   │
       │ job satisfaction experienced           │
       └────────────────────────────────────────┘
                  ↓    ↓    ↓
              ┌──────────────────────┐
              │ **Teacher-task match** │
              └──────────────────────┘
```

According to this scheme, the more closely those items under (b) are matched to those under (a) prior to appointment, or become adapted to them on the job, the better will be the match between teacher and task.

Applying this scheme to the teacher in the present context, three possible points of weakness may be identified. First, the teacher's initial training may have been capable of anticipating rather little of the current job requirements. Second, as already pointed out, the demands of the present work environment may differ significantly from those previously experienced. Third, the selection procedure applied may take insufficient cognisance of the specific conditions obtaining in the school in question. These weaknesses could well lead to an inadequate match between teacher and task in some cases, thus placing a very high premium on personal resourcefulness and adaptability.

Returning to the observed situation, a number of those problems identified in 1984 were still reported as persisting in 1991: e.g. inadequate preparation for the problems of adapting to a European School; differences in national styles of teaching and examining; isolation of the schools; teachers who are unable to teach their mother tongue as a second language; too much reliance on teaching facts rather than analytical thinking; teachers who 'know their subject but cannot teach it'; and French teachers who are still perceived by some as having too 'teacher-centred' a style of teaching. Since the 1991 questionnaire was administered to a limited sample of pupils and parents, however, it is not possible to regard this as representing the views of all in a scientific manner.

Nevertheless it is encouraging to find that a number of ameliorative measures were also reported as having been initiated in the intervening years with reference to the teachers. Recalling those noted above, the chief relevant ones were the institution of in-service training for all the teachers, the appointment of subject co-ordinators, and the move to limit teacher secondment to a maximum of nine years. Besides, the major problem of divergent national styles of teaching and examining, though still matters of complaint by parents and pupils, may now be less sharply defined.

But it would be unbalanced to leave this section without going beyond problems and possible solutions. Credit must be given to the teachers for the achievements that have been attributed to them in submissions received. The 'cultivation of a truly European spirit of tolerance towards other nationalities', the 'undogmatic avoidance of nationalistic tendencies', and 'the cultivation of a wider geopolitical perspective than is found in many of those who have been educated in any national system' were all specified. The readiness of some class teachers to develop and co-operate with remedial teachers, and to carry a pupil counselling role, were also mentioned. Among the major achievements attributed to them were success in language teaching, effectiveness in teaching together pupils of many different cultural backgrounds, a willingness to experiment with new pedagogical techniques, and to contribute to curriculum reform.

Schools, of course, are more than places where information is dispensed, just as educating is much more than formally instructing. The concept of the teacher as having a pastoral role *in loco parentis, vis-à-vis* the pupil, may be a time-honoured one, but it is not one that is shared equally widely among the school systems of the EU Member States. In some schools and school systems, it is formally acknowledged and embodied explicitly in school structures which have the full support of the authorities, while in others a much more limited concept of the teacher's role prevails.

While the writer has observed both didactic and pastoral emphases, side by side in the European Schools, it is felt that the latter may need to be even further encouraged by the authorities here, notwithstanding the appointment of 'subject co-ordinators' in all, as well as a voluntary counselling service for pupils in one School. Indeed, as of 1995 the latter service is now reported to be extending to all the Schools.

Lastly, in view of the growing mobility of teachers from one EU Member State to another, especially since the issuing of the Directive on Teacher Mobility in 1992, some of the problems encountered in the European Schools may well have implications outside this system, whether for migrant teachers (e.g. teachers encountering different employment conditions and practices) or for host schools and school systems (e.g. teachers who are qualified to teach their mother tongue in their own country – but not as a second language). This point is discussed more fully in Chapter 5.

THE PARENTS

The second major group comprising the School community are the parents, and some of these have been among the most vociferous supporters and critics of the European Schools over the years. They have been accorded an important role at several levels in the life of the School; it was, after all, on the initiative of parents that the first European School was set up.

A school does not exist in isolation. Teachers are linked to parents by their children, for whom they both share responsibility. In any school, therefore, probably the most important outside agents on a day-to-day basis are the pupils' parents.

There is no substitute for the knowledge which they have of their own children – even their teachers will never come to know them as fully; but it is often crucially important that the teachers come to share some of it. Knowledge of the individual child's adjustment within the family, of their capacity for making friends, and of any serious difficulty encountered in their developmental or medical history – all would have a bearing on how the teacher should deal with them and help them learn. In the case of expatriate families, the teacher should be made aware of the language or languages of the home, especially if these differ from the dominant school language, of any difficulty experienced by the pupil in adapting to a new environment, and of the configuration of the family in so far as this may affect school work. In the smaller schools, teachers are likely to get to know many of the parents very well through frequent social contact, both groups being members of a small expatriate community. However, this may not happen in the larger schools.

Parents for their part will need to be fully informed of the nature and mission of the European School, its structure into language sections, its unusual curriculum, and its *rites de passage,* any of which may be unfamiliar to them. They will be particularly concerned about continuity in their child's education, first at the point of entry to the school – whether there will be too great a gap or too much repetition of work already done – and again at the point of departure, which frequently precedes re-entry into the home country's school or university system. They will also be concerned to know what academic demands will be made if they enrol their child in a European School, e.g. by the second language requirement in early primary schooling, and by the *langue véhiculaire* policy, either of which may well be a stumbling block for some. The supply of clear and full information from school to home is therefore essential, and each School goes to considerable lengths to produce regular bulletins, as well as information booklets *ad parentes,* presenting details of requirements and demands.

Today in most European countries parents are very likely to keep themselves well informed of educational developments in general. Besides information, they demand a voice in the shaping of their child's schooling. They seek closer contact with the school and are often willing to make considerable sacrifices by placing their resources or talents at the school's disposal in the interest of their child's education. In the process of the field work for the present study, for instance, the writer found parents throughout the Schools, whether as elected representatives or acting on their own initiative, very willing to answer time-consuming questionnaires or to submit to lengthy interviews regarding their experiences of the school in question, thus illustrating the depth of their commitment to their child's education.

Divergent National Traditions

Parents who come from widely scattered parts of the European Union are heirs to very different traditions in maintaining relationships, informal and formal, between school and home. These differences are well documented in sources such as the wide-ranging survey by Macbeth *et al,* (1982), and although they are changing at present, a brief look at some will provide a useful perspective.

Toward one end of the scale lie countries such as Holland and Denmark in which the participation of the local community, and especially of the parents, in the life of the school, has been powerfully institutionalised. Toward the other end lie traditions such as those of Britain and Ireland where quite a different set of attitudes has prevailed. In Britain, McLean (1990) holds, 'there has been a tradition of hostility between parents and school teachers dating from the introduction of compulsory schooling', while Beattie (1978) maintains that formal parental involvement in schools in England and Wales was almost non-existent prior to the Taylor Report of 1977. Likewise in Ireland, Kelly (1970) had noted a low to non-existent level of parental involvement, although Macbeth's findings indicate that things in Ireland and Britain have been improving to a limited degree in more recent years. In Ireland the establishment of School Boards with parent representation is mandatory. National Parent Councils have been set up and these have already distinguished themselves as an articulate and independent voice, in addition to those of the state, churches and teacher unions, in policy-making fora.

In England and Wales things are no doubt also changing in the aftermath of the 1988 Act, though McLean's view (1990) that this, in effect, makes the parents 'the watchdogs of standards of attainment' by pitting neighbouring schools against each other, while giving parents freedom of choice of schools for their children, does not augur too well for healthy teacher-parent partnerships developing in those schools.

Back on continental Europe, however, one of the most remarkable phenomena of school education has been the rapid growth of formal mechanisms for direct parental involvement in school governance. This is true, for example in postwar France especially following the *Loi Haby* of 1975, in Italy since the mid-1970s also, and Germany where, although there had been a Parents' Council (*Elternbeirat*) in every school in Prussia since 1919, the post World War II policy of the Allies gave a very powerful boost to this process of democratisation in education through the *Mitbestimmungsgesetz* (co-determination law).

An interesting though limited comparative study by Pritchard

(1981) illustrates the contrast in this regard between two EU Member States, Germany and Ireland, and their divergent outcomes. From her research findings, she inferred that, while the more formal roles of parents (on class and school councils) in Germany, and the greater parent-teacher contact that is usual there, may impose a degree of strain on the teachers of their children, this nevertheless seemed to be associated with a more favourable attitude on the part of the pupils towards their teachers than in the (then) absence of such councils in Ireland. Second, the German teachers showed more favourable attitudes towards parents than did their Irish counterparts. 'Too little contact leaves the teacher feeling isolated and unsupported by the home; too much contact and observability makes him feel threatened' is Pritchard's conclusion. In short, adequate formal and informal home-school liaison, through making school life more dynamic for teacher and pupil alike, can have important educational outcomes. Notwithstanding the political minefield that it sometimes becomes, legislation to clarify roles, as well as to encourage the growth of mutual respect between parent and teacher, is essential for success.

Parents' Contribution in the European Schools

In view of their diversity, it can be expected that those parents whose children attend any given European School will bring a disparate range of expectations to bear on it, with regard to curriculum, pedagogy and home-school liaison. Nevertheless their contribution to the life of these Schools, both formal through their representatives, and informal through personal contributions, has been an immense and admirable one. As we saw in Chapter 1, at school level they organise the efficient daily network of school buses, which is all-important for a scattered school community. They also play a leading role in the arrangement of school trips, such as *classes de neige* in winter, while the organisation of the school canteen, schoolbook sales and some school entertainment events also owes much to their initiative. While it is the case that many of the teachers will also be parents of children at the School where they teach, and in this sense they can influence the curriculum, nevertheless the major formal channel of such influence for parents *qua* parents will be through their representatives on School Committees.

Given that the European School may be the only educational facility available for some parents without breaking up the family unit, added to the other exigencies of expatriate status, it is not surprising that many parents will hold strong views on their child's school. Their voice has been heard on all major occasions throughout the Schools' history, including the European Parliament Committee Hearing in 1986 and again in the pages of *Schola Europaea*.

In the same year the combined Headmasters, in a report to a Governing Board Working Party, sounded a reassuring, indeed almost complacent, note on relations with the parents, as follows:

> Much of the strength of the European School lies in the concern and energetic interest of the parent body. Elected parents already play a full part in the life of the European Schools as observers at the meetings of the Governing Body, as full voting partners on the administrative boards of individual Schools, and on the Education Committees of the Schools. We see no case for making changes and none has been made to us. (Headmasters 1984)

Each of the European Schools has a similar network of formal parent-teacher communication procedures, viz. school reports, parent-teacher meetings, and teachers making themselves available for individual consultation by parents, with further meetings, usually at the opening of the school year.

Nevertheless, parents' representatives' responses to the present writer's enquiry of 1991 showed some ambivalence regarding consultation with them. It was reported to be better at the level of Boards of Governors and of Inspectors than at that of individual schools.

Again, there may be lessons to be learned from the European Schools' experience by those parents who, in growing numbers, are deciding, for career-related reasons for instance, to move their family to another EU Member State. Expectations of School facilities may not be fulfilled in the host country. School systems differ, sometimes widely, from country to country, and the differences encountered may be difficult to comprehend, or may even become an unacceptable stumbling block to some parents.

In 1984 the criticisms of the Schools most frequently made by parents' representatives to the writer, concerned the teachers, e.g. their problems of adaptation; different national teaching styles; 'tendency to remain too long'. Other points of contention were the high rate of pupil dropout, the students' heterogeneity of cultural background, and the Schools' 'exclusively academic' orientation. Seven years later, in the 1991 enquiry, their major preoccupations showed little change. Again the Schools' 'exclusively academic' orientation came first, inadequacy of guidance on higher education was second, while the teachers' different national styles of teaching came third in frequency of mention. Divergences in teaching and marking as between the language sections, inadequate physical accommodation in some schools, and insufficient help for pupils with learning difficulties also featured in 1991. Nevertheless, the introduction of remedial teaching, enhanced choice of subjects in the Baccalaureate, and the 'truly European and unprejudiced attitudes of pupils' were points of improvement noted by the parents in 1991.

THE PUPILS

Following a steady growth throughout four decades, the combined pupil enrolment of the European Schools now stands at about 15,000. Despite assumptions often made by observers about the homogeneity of their families' social status, the pupils in the various Schools actually represent a very wide range of intellectual, cultural and educational backgrounds, while their range of national and linguistic origins would be difficult to exceed anywhere. Though fewer in the smaller schools, there were children of 40 nationalities speaking 36 or so languages in one of the Brussels Schools in 1984. If we also take into account the normal range of individual differences in rates of intellectual, emotional and physical growth, we begin to gain some idea of the complexity of their pupil population in human terms. Here we look first at pupil-related problems reported to the author, at some aspects of pupil background, and at the educational implications of these. Changing patterns of pupil enrolment are then considered, followed by a discussion of pupils' perspectives on their School.

Pupil-related Problems

The diminishing enrolment of 'entitled' pupils was one of the most frequently reported problems encountered in the 1984 study. Others frequently mentioned both then and in 1991 were the heterogeneity of pupils' cultural/linguistic backgrounds; too many weaker pupils failing and being required to leave; insufficient facilities for pupil guidance and counselling; the wide range of achievement standards among late-enrolling pupils, and some pupils' inability to understand their teachers' language medium in the classroom. The persistence of these problems across the intervening years was somewhat surprising, despite certain ameliorative measures that had been initiated in the interim. However the benefits of the latter were beginning to be felt by 1991.

Background Considerations

The pupils of the European Schools share the same lifestyles, attitudes, aspiration and enthusiasms as many other young Europeans of today, responding in their individual ways to rapidly changing environments. However, in their case, as in the case of highly mobile, cosmopolitan communities elsewhere, certain patterns may become accentuated, others muted, by virtue of their particular situation, growing up and attending school as expatriates.

First, they will frequently have had to accustom themselves to living away from their homeland and adapting to new surroundings in the host country. Being expatriate, though often exciting at first, can also be stressful. This may apply even to very mobile families, especially those who may not speak the language of the host community. In such cases indeed it may be the children who, through school and friends, acquire the new language more rapidly than their parents, while friendships may arise more from school than from home contacts.

Commonly enjoying a high standard of living and material resources, these children may nevertheless experience more frequently the unavoidable absence of one or both parents, resulting in a lot of unsupervised leisure time, with further difficulties arising from both.

Alternatively, such children sometimes may be overprotected because of parental apprehension about an environment which is strange to them. Here a sheltered upbringing may make it difficult for them to acquire the level of independence appropriate to their age. Distance from school and a long school day can exacerbate such effects.

These children frequently come from culturally complex families, with parents of different nationalities and linguistic backgrounds. Some will have experienced the trauma of parental divorce, will now live with a single parent, or share their time between two separated parents. In addition to life in a strange environment, the impact of such disruptions on the growing personality can give rise to further and sometimes serious difficulty for their teachers.

Even within a sedentary community, those children whose parents' jobs lead to very frequent changes of family abode may show more signs of emotional disturbance and poor academic performance than normal. This varies, however, depending on the specific circumstances of the migrant group, on expectations held of them by the host community, and on differences between schools in the country of origin and those in the new environment (Wall 1977). It is not clear whether it is the frequent changes of school as such, or social and cultural factors in the home or the school, that tend to lead to the problems observed, since in one review almost as many studies of school change and reading achievement, for instance, found a positive correlation between them as those reporting a negative one (Swan 1974).

The most obvious educational problems to affect migrant children derive from cultural, social, curricular and organisational differences encountered in the new school. Fundamental divergences in views of what knowledge is essential for children to learn, as well as in expectations of the kinds of relationships encountered in school and classroom, could be no more than sources of amusement in some instances, but of sharp conflict in others.

Children in migrant families who are subjected to frequent interruptions of schooling, with consequent disruption of friendships, and adaptation to new friends, new teachers and new environments, can suffer emotionally and educationally unless special counteracting steps are taken, although in the majority of cases these problems seem more likely to be transitory than permanent.

Sheridan (1978) carried out a psychological study of two groups of middle- to upper-class adolescent girls of different national origins, one of them at school in Rome and the other in California, in order to assess the effect of relative stability or change of environment on their personality development. The major finding was that the 'transient' adolescent was more trusting, more affected by feelings, more easily upset and with less ego strength than her culture-bound counterpart. She also seemed more vulnerable, less secure and less emotionally self-sufficient. The researcher found it logical that she should be more trusting since her dependence on others becomes greater as she moves from country to country. Besides, while the overseas student may be, or may appear to be, more sophisticated and more in command of the situation, the evidence produced here suggested that in fact she was less secure, less self-reliant and less uninhibited. Since this study was not longitudinal, it shed no light on the important question of whether these features were merely transitory or of longer duration. However, without generalising unduly from one limited study, it does seem possible that the 'transient' adolescent fears having to leave her friends again, not being admitted into new peer groups, not being accepted for what he or she is. It is important therefore that parents, teachers and educational planners realise that these adolescents may be more vulnerable emotionally than their less mobile peers.

Other groups which may encounter serious difficulties as a result of migration to radically different environments are those who already have specific or general learning difficulties. All this can throw considerable burdens of demand and expectation back on the teacher, not only for the cognitive and academic, but also for the emotional and social development of the pupil. School is now called upon to be a reference point, a place of security and meaning, of advice and support beyond what would normally be expected, with teachers sometimes cast in the role of surrogate parents.

With regard to the psycho-educational counselling of expatriate children showing emotional problems, it is relevant to note here that cultural differences between the client and the counsellor have been found to create barriers to effective counselling. Such features as not sharing a common mother tongue, major discrepancies between them in values, attitudes, beliefs and expectations, as well as differences in non-verbal communication, can play havoc with the actual reception of the intended message, while differences in underlying values, e.g. an emphasis on the individual rather than on the family or group, could also contribute to difficulties in the counsellor-client relationship (Fitzgerald and O'Leary 1990).

School Structure and Pupil Enrolment Patterns

Each School has a kindergarten, primary and secondary department. It will be recalled from Chapter 1 that the pupil enrolment in the combined Schools totalled 15,058 in August 1994 (see Table 1.1).

A pupil may enrol in the kindergarten or nursery section between the ages of four and six; transfer into primary occurs in the year of their sixth birthday and, following the successful completion of the primary course or another accepted as equivalent, they are normally admitted to secondary in the year of their eleventh birthday. Late-arriving pupils may be admitted subject to certain conditions, but in view of the demands of the curriculum, the earlier in their school career they arrive, the more successful they are likely to be.

Changes in Pupil Numbers

The pattern of growth already noted has been particularly strong in certain Schools, especially in both those in Brussels, and those in Munich, Karlsruhe, Culham and Bergen. Indeed the two largest schools, now numbering over 3,000 pupils each, apart from being reported as seriously overcrowded, are regarded by some parents as unacceptably large school units in themselves.

However, the school by school analysis given in Table 4.3 shows that the pattern of growth marks an actual decline over the five-year period 1984-89 in the School at Varese, though this has now been almost completely overcome, while that in Mol had lost numbers to a serious extent in the same period. This seems to derive from a lack of ability on the part of these particular Schools to attract sufficient numbers of 'non-entitled' pupils to fill those places not taken up by 'entitled' families associated with the EU institutions or research centres in the vicinity of each.

Table 4.3   Changes in Pupil Enrolments 1984-89

School	% Total Pupil Population Change
Luxembourg	+16
Brussels I	+22
Brussels II	+24
Mol	−23
Varese	−1
Karlsruhe	+35
Bergen	+18
Munich	+37
Culham	+26

As Table 4.3 shows, apart from Varese and Mol, there had been quite a robust growth in numbers in all the remaining Schools, suggesting a buoyant interest and demand for this type of education.

Since the admissions policy of the Schools has a direct bearing on the composition of the pupil population and has been criticised on a number of occasions, e.g. in the Peus Report (European Parliament 1986), it is important that we evaluate this policy in the light of changing conditions.

The Digest of Decisions of the Board of Governors (14th Edition, page 120) informs us that in formulating the *General Rules* the Board adopted these criteria for the admission of new pupils:

1. The following are automatically admitted:
   - children of the staff of the Institutions of the European Community
   - children of staff of organisations with which the Board of Governors has already concluded an agreement (based on Article 5 of the Protocol on the setting up of the European Schools).
2. The following are admitted with priority:
   - other children of nationals of the European Community Member States.
3. The following can also be admitted:
   - children from countries outside the Community.

Admissions under 2 and 3 above are possible, provided accommodation and places are available without classes having to be divided, and in return for the payment of relatively modest fees; as we have seen, it has become customary to refer to these as 'non-entitled' pupils, whereas those admitted under category 1 are known as 'entitled' pupils. This explains why there are small numbers of 'non-entitled' children in locations such as Brussels and Luxembourg where there is a high density of EU officials, and why there are far higher percentages of 'non-entitled' pupils elsewhere.

Looking at the pattern of 'entitled' enrolments on the other hand over a recent five-, and again ten-year period, we find that Luxembourg was the only School whose percentage of 'entitled' pupils had actually increased, and this one may have 'peaked' in

1983-84. Table 4.4 illustrates.

It will be seen from Table 4.4 that (i) the rate of decline had increased in Varese, had slowed somewhat in Mol and Karlsruhe, and had remained more or less constant in Bergen and Culham; (ii) that in five of these Schools, less than half of all pupils were now 'entitled'; in Bergen about one in five; in Karlsruhe about one in eight, a trend that has continued since then.

Table 4.4   'Entitled' Pupils as a Percentage of Enrolments over 10 Years

		Years	
School	1979/80	1983/84	1989/90
Luxembourg	72	88	85
Brussels I	73	65	71
Brussels II	87	83	83
Mol	55	37	30
Varese	84	78	44
Karlsruhe	34	18	13
Bergen	53	38	22
Munich	73	67	64
Culham	57	48	37

Two conclusions may be drawn. First that in the smaller Schools the viability of the smaller language-sections becomes uncertain, a problem which could persist, even with increasing numbers of 'non-entitled', while the range of subjects offered within those smaller language-sections had also diminished. The second conclusion is that, when this happens, one of the major aims of the schools is thwarted, in that a continuous education through the mother tongue from nursery to school-leaving can no longer be guaranteed to the children of certain national groups.

Pupil Status and Parental Choice

Even under settled demographic conditions any school is liable to experience fluctuations in pupil numbers, while the recent or current decline in the child population of many European countries has presented their authorities with major administrative headaches in educational provision. Nevertheless the problem of the European Schools is *sui generis,* and must be examined in its particular context. It is said that the average age of officials of the European Union and its related institutions is now advancing, and that the proportion of children of schoolgoing age in these families is therefore declining. This may well be one cause of the problem in question.

But we should also look at the context of each School, especially the availability of satisfactory alternatives, and ask how many of those parents who are employed by an EU-related institution, and who do have an alternative, are in fact choosing a European School for their child? One study carried out at the end of 1982, and confined to the Brussels area, showed the position as it was then. The findings are given in Table 4.5.

Table 4.5   Percentage Enrolment at a European School 1982

Nationality	%
Belgian	9
British	57
Danish	73
Dutch	57
French	43
German	56
Greek	54
Irish	74
Italian	56
Luxembourg	67

The indications then were that considerable majorities of Belgian and French parents were choosing an alternative school, of which there would be many in their language in the Brussels area. On the other hand, substantial majorities of Danish, Irish and Luxembourg parents were choosing a European School, but whether on its merits or because they had no alternative is not known.

A further study carried out at the end of 1983, and cited in the Peus Report to the European Parliament, found that 60 per cent of the 4,604 children of Commission Officials in Brussels were enrolled in Schools other than a European School and that the percentage attending the Schools had fallen from 52 per cent in 1973 to 40 per cent in 1983. This study enquired into the reasons for this by means of a questionnaire. The main reasons given, in order of relative frequency, were as follows:

1. Distance between home and school.
2. Lack of discipline in the School, whether observed or inferred from reputation.
3. Teachers' lack of commitment.
4. The nature of the syllabus, and lower academic standards, especially in Science, mother tongue and Mathematics.
5. Schools' bilingual policy unacceptable.
6. Schools too narrowly academic in outlook and syllabus, with insufficient attention being paid to music and the plastic arts.
7. No alternative examination to Baccalaureate then available in the Schools.[1]
8. National schools were preferred, whether in the host or in the home country.
9. The parents' desire for admission to kindergarten of children below age four, for a genuine religious education, or for boarding schools.
10. Other considerations.

In response to these findings, Dr Peus's Report called for a new definition of 'entitled' pupils and, while emphasising that a European School cannot be open to *all* immigrants, nevertheless described as 'ideal' the proposal of the Commission in 1974 that the system be 'open to children of all EEC nationalities *without distinction*' (p.3) (emphasis added).

A Dilemma of Policy

The serious decline in 'entitled' pupils in all but three of the Schools presented the authorities with a critical dilemma. Should they not, as recommended in the Peus Report, liberalise their admissions policy towards, for instance, admitting all children of EU Member States' citizens at least, on an equal basis – assuming there are plenty of such applying? This policy, if practicable, would help the viability of the Schools in question; but it would not be feasible in Brussels, or in Luxembourg where there are considerable accommodation problems at present.

But to do this beyond a certain point seems likely to give rise to another problem. Would it sooner or later change the character of the Schools in question so that they would become indistinguishable from any of the national schools in the district and, in that event, would the various authorities continue to fund them as before? Or could a sufficient range of language-sections and other features be maintained so as to ensure that it remained a European School?

Perhaps it is not a simple 'either-or' problem but rather the interaction of size with heterogeneity that is important. It will be a matter of judgment when the critical level, which jeopardises the viability of any School, has been reached. Already, indeed, with quite small minorities of 'entitled' pupils in three Schools, this question must have occurred to the authorities, but it seems likely that a new balance between the ideal and the emerging reality may have to be sought in the future.

An alternative solution towards ensuring the future of the system might be sought by way of setting up further European Schools in other locations where there is a concentration of families from a number of EU Member States, whether related to an EU institution or not. This was proposed by Mr Van Houtte, one of the main progenitors of the concept of European Schools, in his response to the Peus Report. But the official position on this, as set forth in a communication from the Commission, is that 'the general policy of the Board of Governors is to create new Schools only at the request of institutions of the European Community, and not at that of other international institutions (except the European Patent Organisation in Munich, in which the Community has a special interest).' Presumably this means that any movement away from this position would require a totally new intergovernmental agreement.

Two recent innovations seem likely to alleviate the position in the Schools concerned. First, individual Schools have begun in recent years to enter into agreement with specific institutions or firms in their area, whereby places will be guaranteed for children of their employees, in return for the payment of the full unsubsidised school fee.

The second is the concept of *'enfant libre'*, whereby children who come to live in the vicinity for a short period are being admitted to a School at the Director's discretion, on the understanding that they will not be remaining to take the Baccalaureate examination. In fact it is not difficult usually to 'build' an individual programme from existing curricular elements, in order to help such a pupil benefit while attending the school.

Neither the issue of shifting enrolments as between 'entitled' and 'non-entitled' pupils, nor similar issues bearing on the future viability of particular schools, was addressed directly in the 1994 Statute. However Article 30 states that the Board of Governors may negotiate with the government of a country in which a School is located any additional agreement required to ensure that the School can operate under the best possible conditions. This could leave open several possibilities, including the establishment of boarding facilities, should this be deemed appropriate.

Pupils' Perspective on their School

How then do the pupils perceive and respond to their school experience? From the responses of their representatives both in 1984 and in 1991, there emerges a strong impression, at least from the larger Schools, that they see their School not so much as a single cohesive institution, but rather as a conglomerate of several different linguistic/national schools under one roof. And yet they do make friends across the different language sections and break down the language 'barriers' with increasing ease as they move up the grades. As shown in the study by Blomme *et al.* (1989) of the School in Bergen, and reported by several interviewees to the present writer, they also seem to 'become in mind European', acquiring a European consciousness or dimension of their identity, whether from School, from home, or both.

While it is impossible to say how far one can generalise from this to the other Schools, small or large, it is worthwhile focusing on this study as a unique source of pupils' reflections. One of its findings is that 'the [degree of] integration is so good that it is difficult to adapt to your own country when you return', in the words of a German ex-pupil. On the whole the authors of that study felt that the verdict of those pupils who had represented the period 1976 to 1987 was positive or, where negative, it was nevertheless constructively so. The fluency in several languages, the breadth of the curriculum, and the good grounding given in Mathematics were among the achievements identified there. On the negative side, they did highlight the difficulty of 'how to ensure that integration does not simply mean the assimilation of the "weakest" into the "strongest"' (Blomme *et al.* 1989, p.22).

The specific problems most frequently reported by pupils to this writer to 1984 focused on the following: teachers 'who know their subject but cannot teach it'; a generation gap between teacher and pupil; and insufficient careers guidance. 'A "teacher-centred" approach on the part of French teachers', 'the use of the *langue véhiculaire* in teaching Human Sciences', 'teaching for memory rather than analytical thinking', and difficulties related to 'the Reform' (the process of curriculum review in the Schools) – were also specified as problems.

Each of these also recurred in 1991, as well as differences in marking systems between language-sections, the use of national texts, pupils' narrow range of social experience, and what was enigmatically described by one respondent as 'problems of criminality and vandalism'. Nevertheless the 'immediate acceptance of friends from different backgrounds', the widespread acceptability of the European Baccalaureate, and lastly the 'undogmatic avoidance of nationalist tendencies' were all reported by pupils' representatives as advantages of the European Schools, or as matters where the national school systems could learn a lesson from them. Lastly, it should be noted here that the 'Reform' Committee has been brought to an end by the 1994 legislation.

Dropout of Pupils from the Schools

The turnover of pupils in the European Schools is considerable, as might be expected in a rather mobile population. Naturally there are many who arrive at some point after their schooling has begun, and it seems that any admitted after grades 5 or 6 are more likely to have serious difficulties in adjusting to this particular curriculum.

Each School publishes annual statistics which give data on and general reasons for departures – how many leave for 'scholastic' and how many for 'personal' or other (unspecified) reasons. It is not easy to know how such data are to be interpreted. Of those who left these Schools in the year 1989, the percentage doing so for scholastic reasons, or to go to another school, ranged from 8.8 per cent to 45 per cent across the Schools. Since any school failure may have elements contributed by the pupil as well as the teacher, how much of it would be prevented by better schooling is a question each School and its staff members must answer for themselves, in any individual instance.

The high dropout rate was a source of complaint by some parent, teacher and School Director representatives in 1984; it figured again in 1991. The procedure of 'counselling out' weak pupils or those who fail examinations was also identified as a problem in both enquiries; in the words of one senior School teacher, 'we are redirecting our failures into the national school systems'. Certainly many teachers and Directors saw this as a major shortcoming of the system, while parents' representatives were also seriously concerned.

CONCLUSION

This chapter delineates the human complexity of the European Schools as a system, and the likelihood of consequent problems. The teachers, pupils and parents were aware of the benefits of this kind of schooling, but also of the problems, and there was no real indication of complacency among them.

The Board of Governors has undertaken ameliorative measures

in recent years, the effects of which are becoming apparent. At secondary level pupils have benefited from the extended subject choice in the Baccalaureate from harmonising the Fifth-Year Programme, the Intermediate Evaluation and, in 1995, significantly enhanced funding for Career Guidance facilities in each School. At primary level, remedial teaching in all schools is helping quite a lot of those with learning difficulties, while the admission of a small number with handicapping conditions is also to the credit of the authorities, as long as their specific educational needs are met – not an easy task in such a complex school environment.

Chapter 5

THE EUROPEAN SCHOOLS – THEIR ACHIEVEMENTS, PROBLEMS AND WIDER SIGNIFICANCE

The problems of living together on this continent at this time set new goals for basic education, but the extent to which these can be attained depends on the role assigned to the school.

T. Husén, A. Tuijnman and W. D. Halls (1992)

We must be still and still moving
Into a further intensity
For a further union, a deeper communion.

T.S. Eliot: *Four Quartets* (1944)

In this final chapter a brief academic audit of the effectiveness of the European Schools is presented, and their broader significance for education in Europe and in general is assessed. While the Schools must go on learning and developing themselves, it is also concluded that their unique experiences do anticipate or reflect serious and growing problems in other European school systems and could, if shared, enrich education elsewhere in Europe and indeed worldwide as we move into the new millennium.

Achievements

The respondents to the writer's enquiries, especially to the questionnaire of 1991, identified the breadth of their curriculum, their language-teaching policies, and their cultivation of tolerant, unprejudiced attitudes towards others, as the three greatest pedagogical achievements of the European Schools. To these were added the cultivation of a specifically European mentality or identity and the replacing of cultural *assimilation* with cultural *pluralism* in education, within the European family of nations. The historic breakthrough of the founders was to relocate the education of the young on a truly multinational plane, while continuing to serve its national purposes. The great achievement of their teachers is to show that this is possible, and is frequently being achieved to the highest educational standards, whilst eliding the perception of each other as foreigners, among young Europeans. This is a first step towards achieving Goethe's ideal „damit ihm zu Hause kein Fremder unbequem, er aber in der Fremde überall zu Hause ist" (that no stranger ever feel himself unwelcome in his home, nor he himself a stranger anywhere throughout the world).

Problems

On the other hand, the major pedagogical problems identified by the respondents to the same enquiries were the Schools' continuing academic selectivity, and the divergent approaches to pedagogy and examinations that have persisted between the different language sections or cultural groups. A shortage of appropriate textbooks, the relative isolation of the Schools, insufficient preparation of teachers, and the underdeveloped state of pupil support services (e.g. remedial teaching, pupil counselling, and pastoral care) in a number of the Schools, were also highlighted.

Two further questions sought indications of ways in which the European Schools and the national systems in general might each learn from the other. The respondents felt that the Schools' deployment of native speakers to teach foreign languages and the provision of a multilingual environment were strategies that could usefully be adopted from them by others; the introduction of greater school autonomy and a middle management (e.g. Heads of Department) structure, were useful innovations which, it was felt, the European Schools in turn might adopt from some national systems.

As to whether the European Schools' system as a whole has been a success or a failure, this issue was raised with the writer in a submission from the Parents' Committee of the Brussels II School in 1984 and may have been implicit in the Oostlander report outlined in Chapter 1. The argument in the former case was based on (i) the perceived 'programme-centred' pedagogy of the Schools, (ii) the multi-subject Baccalaureate as against the three subject GCE A-levels in the UK, and (iii) the fact that the Schools did not cater for the needs of Community officials as a whole, including those who chose not to send their children to them in the first place.

However, to take the last point first, there could be perfectly acceptable reasons (e.g. distance from home, or the availability of preferred local alternatives) for parents so deciding, although there is evidence of such choices in some cases also amounting to a vote of no confidence in the European Schools. It is not possible to quantify the choices in either case, but disquiet among a minority of parents about the Schools' failure to cater adequately for weaker pupils has persisted.

In fact there can be no single answer to the issue of the overall 'success' or 'failure' of the Schools, and such comments as those given above probably reflect the cultural background of the commentator. Even ten years ago a 'child-centred' pedagogy was, at least officially, in vogue in many countries, but it would find less favour today in some of those same countries. Secondly the unfavourable comparison of the Baccalaureate with the A-levels in England, Wales and Northern Ireland is less convincing when one realises that most EU Member States, including Scotland and Ireland, favour a broader and (more or less) balanced programme of at least five, but often far more, subjects at senior secondary level itself. This is not to say that any one tradition is 'right' or 'wrong', but that preferences in education are more often based on value judgments, which in turn arise out of one's own cultural imperatives. But with twelve sets of such imperatives converging in one institution, and pressing choices to be made among them, it is inevitable that some will feel vindicated, others defeated, on this issue or that. To generalise, however tempting it may be, from one's own personal experience to those of all the rest, as seems to have happened in that 1984 submission, would therefore be invalid; indeed, paradoxically the same document itself maintained that 'the European Schools system is basically no better or no worse than other systems'.

Future Prospects

From these findings there emerges the image of a network of schools that is successful in many ways in achieving its unique goals, but one that is still evolving. In particular, throughout the ten-year period of this study, certain divergences have persisted between the language-sections, in the view of some parents, teachers and pupils, which the harmonised curriculum has not overcome. Clearly efforts must continue towards developing a coherent and rounded philosophy of schooling, matched to their unique mission, as well as to the exigencies of the population they serve, and drawing on the most advanced educational experience of the day.

At the same time, it seems necessary to call for a new balance between central and local direction of these Schools, towards giving each one a somewhat greater measure of autonomy, coupled with the requirement of developing its own school plan, and making explicit its own objectives within an agreed framework. The provision of a learning environment which will facilitate enhanced autonomy in learning for the individual student would also be in line with current thinking in education as a whole, and the view of one's school years as only the first stage of a lifelong process of learning.

Again, while it is important to work diligently towards closer links with the school systems of those countries where the Schools are located, too close an integration with them could easily lead to the creation of inequalities of esteem within any such European School, which would favour the pupils and teachers of the country of its location above the rest. If this were to happen, one of the unique achievements of these Schools (viz. the cultivation of pluralism instead of assimilation) would immediately be forfeited. Thus, for instance, the School in Varese would become essentially an Italian School, those in Brussels essentially Belgian, and so on.

On the other hand, the prospect of simply adding more and more language-sections to existing Schools with the accession of first more Scandinavian and, in due course, some former Eastern Bloc European countries to the EU, brings closer a problem that may be solved only by a 'variable geometry' model of European School or schooling. The concept of developing foreign language sections within national schools, perhaps with the national governments drawing on the expertise of the European Schools themselves and of such bodies as the Council of Europe, may be worth exploring as a complementary and less cumbersome strategy. Indeed, the opening of bilingual or foreign language sections in schools in some Member States, most notably in Germany (North-Rhine Westphalia and Berlin), France, Holland and Denmark has been in progress since the 1970s. According to Hart, they numbered 80 in Germany alone by 1992 (Hart 1992). Besides these, a growing number of frequently unsung initiatives to introduce a European dimension into the curriculum can be witnessed throughout the national systems of the Member States, most with EU funding, and these seem set to go on growing. Whether they are having any real impact on popular attitudes towards the EU however, or contributing to a feeling of European citizenship, is difficult to say.

Significance

The European Schools' experience has further significance in three respects: first for communication, second for convergence in education, and third for coexistence among the nations of Europe.

The EU comprises several distinct communities of discourse on education and schooling, each having its own language or languages, terminology and conceptual framework. These only partly coincide with nationality or groups of nations. They also have their sub-groups and local variants. But each has in the past been largely self-sustaining, relatively isolated from the others, and indeed the level of mutual incomprehension among them is amazing.

Yet dialogue on and in education must now take place across the barriers that separate these communities; there will not be a European community of education until we recognise and find ways of transcending these barriers. Perhaps the best way of achieving this is by representatives of each system working together in the same schools, side by side.

This of course is what the teachers in the European Schools are doing on a daily basis since these Schools are both *sui generis* and yet organically linked to each national system. They therefore daily become pioneers of communication across these linguistic and conceptual frontiers. As laboratories of innovation, then, and mediators of new ideas, the European Schools could play a powerful role in furthering discourse in education, especially by showing how multicultural perspectives can enrich beyond measure, despite initial barriers to understanding. Besides, communication in and about education is of far more than academic or professional significance; it opens up genuine cultural understanding for the whole younger generation.

Convergence among the public education systems of Europe is no longer a matter of choice, but of necessity, a point on which Nordenbo (1993) takes issue with McLean (1990). Educational concerns transcend not only national but continental boundaries in this world of the instant transmission of images and possibilities, of expectations and problems. At the same time, with costly and ceaseless change washing over our schools, and far more problems than solutions, the European Schools have weathered experiences which, if shared, could help to shed light on some emerging problems among the national school systems. Meeting the educational needs of highly mobile expatriate families, overcoming cultural and language differences and working towards a multinational, in this case European, identity are achievements whose wider sharing would smooth the way for the convergence process. Their experience in the deployment of teachers (and inspectors) from many national systems could add to the European Schools' contribution to convergence.

The case for a common basic European curriculum in the Member States of the EU is self-evident to many observers, especially teachers in schools and universities whose classes comprise increasing numbers of expatriates. Workers and professionals, parents and pupils even still cross frontiers with some trepidation about the education ahead, despite the promise of the Maastricht Treaty and the Single European Act before it. Their anxiety often proves to be well-founded; but this cannot be allowed to continue. They need to travel secure in the knowledge that their valid qualifications will be recognised, and that their children will receive a comparable education anywhere in the European Union. Europe is on the move, and schools must move with it. Travel, trade and the electronic media have broken down geographical barriers. It is now up to education to remove barriers of a cultural, conceptual and sometimes bureaucratic nature. Having extended the boundaries of the possible, e.g. with the widespread automatic recognition now accorded to the European Baccalaurate, the European Schools' experience could become a catalyst for changing structures and processes of schooling in the Member States.

Yet inevitable though convergence among the school systems of the EU may be, some fear that it may take the form of the larger States' curricula growing stronger, at the expense of the smaller, e.g. through school certificates and professional diplomas from these more powerful states 'driving out' those of the others, fuelled perhaps by economic domination. If such apprehensions are in fact realistic, then positive, preventative policies at EU level will need to be put in place.

Here especially, the European Schools' experience could be most valuable since, as we know, they have valued diversity, and eschewed domination or assimilation. The deliberate valuing of minority cultures, as well as the cultivation of a common identity (rather than of dominant ones only), is seen as offering the best hope that such an undesirable outcome will not happen, at any rate by default. The European Schools have, sometimes painfully, pioneered pluralism of the kind desired and it would be short-sighted not to build on the foundations they have laid over the past forty years. Direct knowledge of others, such as they have fostered, is a prerequisite to valuing them, while also leading to a deeper appreciation of one's own culture and identity. In view of this, there is much wisdom in Shennan's assertion that 'for the young in Europe today a European education is a political, social and economic necessity, an affirmation of their cultural birthright' (Shennan 1991, p.19). The tendency to view the EU as having no more than economic significance, or to pretend that European Union does not have an educational dimension, is at best short-sighted and restrictive. Both the process of European unification and the experience of instantaneous worldwide communications are challenging educators to reassert the universality of learning in new ways appropriate to its enlarging context – without ceasing to value what is good in the local, the particular or the traditional.

Of course we are still far from solving all our problems of coexistence as peoples, while tensions and even contradictions between national and European loyalties still persist throughout the European Union. Our national school systems, too, march to different drums, with the European dimension a mere after-thought in all too many, and harmonisation between them scarcely mentioned.

Like the EU itself, the great weakness of the European Schools is their sheer diversity; and yet, in both cases, it can also be seen as the greatest source of richness and strength. Caught as they are between different, often conflicting, cultural paradigms, the European Schools' experience of coexistence gives a lead for the parent societies to follow. These Schools have indeed found a new balance between nationalism and Europeanism, between conflicting loyalties and competing identities, which offers the best hope for the future, of bringing into being a united and thriving Europe.

NOTES AND REFERENCES

Chapter 1. THE EUROPEAN SCHOOLS: CONCEPT, CONTROVERSY AND COMMENT

References

Adorno,T.W. (1988): 'Erziehung nach Auschwitz' in *Erziehung zur Mundigkeit*, Frankfurt-M., 88-104; cited by M. Blum, A. Kaplyta, M. Schmitt, E. Weisser, 'Germans and Other Strangers' in B.Kruithof and S.Sting (eds) (1993): *Education and Modernization: The European Experience*, Amsterdam, Network Educational Science (NESA), 50-57.

Blomme, L., C. Maffioli and D. Pickersgill (1989): 'An Assessment of the European School, Bergen by its ex-pupils', *Schola Europaea*, XII, No.105, 5-28.

Bulwer, J.D. (1990): 'Becoming a European: Language and Nationalities in a European School' (mimeo, unpublished).

Clarotti, G. (1994): 'Un futur pour les Ecoles Européennes?', *Euresco*, Nr 5, Premier trimestre.

Delors, J. (1993): Letter of Salutation, *Schola Europaea 1953-1993*, The European School, 80 Rue d'Arlon, 1049 Brussels, p.14.

EEC (1990): Joint Conference of the Commission of the European Communities and the Council for Cultural Co-operation of the Council of Europe: 'Secondary Schools and European/International Education in Europe: Mobility, Curricula and Examinations', Namur, 21-23 May (mimeo, unpublished).

Erikson, E.H. (1968): *Identity, Youth and Crisis*, London, Faber and Faber.

European Commission (1993): The European Schools: Observations on the points raised in the Oostlander Report: 09/1512/93EN.

European Parliament (1983): Debates in the European Parliament, *Verbatim Report of the Proceedings*, No. 1-302/19, 4.7.1983.
European Parliament (1986): *Verbatim Report of the Proceedings*, Strasbourg, 7.4.1986, p.116.
European Parliament (1993): Doc.EN\PR\239\239221: Committee on Culture, Youth, Education and the Media, Draft Report on the Commission Proposal for a Council decision on the conclusion by the European Economic Community and the European Atomic Energy Community of the Convention defining [COM (93) 0061 final - C3-0142/93] Rapporteur: Mr A. M. Oostlander, 15 November 1993.
European Schools (1993): Observations on the points raised by the Oostlander Report: 09/1512/93EN.
FFPE (1991): *Dialogue: Publication de la Féderation de la Fonction Publique Européene: Que se Passe-t-il au sein des Ecoles Européennes?* Nr.1 Juin.
Halls, W. D. (1974): 'Towards a European Education System?', *Comparative Education*, 10, 3, October, 212.
Hart, Michael (1989): 'The Role of the European Schools in the 1990s', *European Journal of Education*, Vol.24, No.2, 197-201.
Lewis, A. (1993): 'What kind of education did I get?', *Schola Europaea 1953-1993*, Brussels, The European School, 80 Rue d'Arlon, pp.116-19.
Mallinson, Vernon (1980): *The European Idea in Education*, Oxford, Pergamon Press, p.372.
Marshall, J. (1987): 'Pressure to Dispel Market Throng', *The Times Educational Supplement*, 21 December 1987.
Melucci, A. (1989): *Nomads of the Present: Social Movements and Individual Needs in Contemporary Society*, London, Hutchinson Radius (cited in P. Schlesinger, q.v.).
Monnet, J. (1962): Letter to A. van Houtte, Representative of the Board of Governors of the European School in Luxembourg, in *Schola Europaea Luxemburgensis*, 1953-1963.
Neave, Guy (1984): *The EEC and Education*, Stock-on-Trent [*sic*], Trentham Books, 1984, p.131.
Oostlander, A.M. (1993): Reaction to the memorandum drawn up by the Commission in response to the Oostlander Report on the European Schools, Doc. EN\DV\242\242598.
Parlement Européen(1993): Commission de la Culture, de la Jeunesse, de l'Education, et des Medias, Annexe IV, 30 Juin Document de Travail, Rapporteur: M. A. Oostlander, Doc. FR\DT\229,229694-PER.
Schlesinger, Philip (1991): *Media State and Nation: Political Violence and Collective Identities*, London, Sage Publications.
Spaak, Paul Henri (1962): Letter to A. Van Houtte, Representative of the Board of Governors of the European School in Luxembourg, in *Schola Europaea Luxemburgensis*, 1953-1963.

Notes and References

Swan, D. (1984): *The European Schools: Crossroads of Education in Europe.* Report of a study carried out for the Commission of the European Communities (unpublished).
Tosi, A. (1991): 'Language in International Education', in P. Jonietz and D. Harris (eds), *World Yearbook of Education 1991: International Schools and International Education,* London, Kogan Page, pp.88-99.
Wathelet, F.(1993): 'Quel type d'education ai-je reçu?', in *Schola Europaea 1953-1993,* Brussels, The European School, 80 Rue d'Arlon, pp.113-16, and 116-19 respectively.

Footnotes

1. On previous occasions the Parliament held debates on the European Schools when the *Merton Report,* doc.8, Resolution OJ No.53 of 24/3/1966, the *Walkoff Report,* doc.113/75, Resolution OJ No.239/11 of 20/10/1975, *Papapietro Report,* doc.1-390/83, Resolution OJ No.C242/81 of 12/9/1983, *Peus Report,* doc.A2-244/86, Resolution OJ No.C125/63 of 7/4/1987 were published. Financial problems featured in the *Kellet-Bowman Report,* doc.1-345/81, Resolution OJ No.234/107 of 10/7/1981, the *Schön Report,* doc.1-333/83, Resolution OJ No. C77/157 of 19/3/1984, the *Schön Interim Report,* doc.A2-180/86, Resolution OJ No. C125/61 of 7/4/1987.
2. There are lessons in which pupils from several language sections are taught together in such activities as arts and crafts, with a view to mitigating the separateness of the language sections from each other in the formal work of the Schools.

Chapter 2.   CURRICULUM AND ASSESSMENT: ELIDING FOREIGNNESS
References
Baetens Beardsmore, H. and M. Swain (1985): 'Designing Bilingual Education', *Journal of Multilingual and Multicultural Education,* Vol.6, No.1, 1-15.
Baetens Beardsmore, H. and J. Kohls (1988): 'Immediate Pertinence in the Acquisition of Multilingual Proficiency: The European Schools (Part 2)', *Schola Europaea,* XII, No.102, 4-12.
Blomme, L., C. Maffioli and D. Pickersgill (1989): 'An Assessment of the European School, Bergen by its ex-pupils', *Schola Europaea,* XII, No.105, 5-28.
Board of Governors of the European Schools (1993): Board of Governors meeting, 26-27 January 1993, summary of reports by the external examiners on the European Baccalaureate, 92-D-248/1, p.11.
Briggs, A. (1988) in M. Hederman (ed.): *The Clash of Ideas, Essays in honour of Patrick Lynch,* Dublin, Gill and Macmillan, p.47.
Broadfoot, P., M. Osborn, A.P. Gilles (1988): 'What Professional Responsibility

Means to Teachers: National Contexts and Classroom Constants', *British Journal of Sociology of Education*, Vol.9, No.3, pp.265-87.
Bulwer, J. (1992): 'Making a Second Language Work', *Cambridge Journal of Education*, Vol.22, No.2, 32-46.
Department of Education and Science (1985): *The European Schools and the European Baccalaureate*, London, DES, p.10. (The writer is indebted to the Department of Education and Science for permission to quote from this work.)
DFE (Department for Education) (1994): *The European Schools and the European Baccalaureate – Guidelines for Universities and Colleges*, London, Department for Education.
Galvin, Richard (1995): Information given to the writer by Mr R. Galvin, a Geography teacher in Brussels I, based on unpublished research on Geography teaching in the European Schools.
Halls, W.D. (1974): 'Towards a European Education System', *Comparative Education*, October, 211-19.
Hart, M. (1992): *The European Dimension in General Primary and Secondary Education*, Alkmaar, The Netherlands: CEVNO (Centre for International Education).
Hart, M. (1994): Summary of the Report by the External Examiners on the 1993 European Baccalaureate, presented to Board of Governors January 1994.
Husband, M. (1983): 'Nursery Education', Report of Working Party under the Chairmanship of Mr Husband, September 1993, EE/2116/83-EN.
International Bureau of Education: *International Yearbook of Education*, Vol.XXXC, 1983, pp.134-89.
Lawton, Denis (1989): *Education, Culture and the National Curriculum*, London, Hodder and Stoughton, p.20.
McGrath, A. (1982): 'The European School in Luxembourg', *The Secondary Teacher*, Vol.11, No.2 (Winter), 17-20.
McLean, Martin (1990): *Britain and a Single Market Europe: Prospects for a Common School Curriculum*, London, Kogan Page with Institute of Education, University of London.
Mickel, W.W. (1986): *The European Dimension in the Classroom*, Alkmaar, The Netherlands: ECN Publications, 1986.
Mikes, G. (1946): *How to be an Alien*, London and New York, Wingate. Quoted in P. Schlesinger (1991), q.v.
Nordenbo, Sven Erik (1993): 'What is implied by a "European Curriculum"?' in B. Kruithof and S. Sting (eds): *Education and Modernization: The European Experience*, Amsterdam, NESA (Network Educational Science), 12-21.
Ó Néill, Pádraig (1990): 'The European Schools', *Oideas – Iris na Roinne Oideachais*, 36, Geimhreadh, 21-35.
Opitz, W. (1990): 'Europädagogik in Europäischen Schulen', *Schola Europaea*,

XII, No.109, 5-14.

Swan, D. (1984): *The European Schools – Crossroads of Education in Europe*, Report to the Commission of the European Communities (unpublished), p.66.

Tosi, A. (1991): 'Language in International Education', in P.L. Jonietz and D. Harris (eds), *World Yearbook of Education 1991: International Schools and International Education*, London, Kogan Page, p.97.

Van der Spek, C. (1994): Geschiedenis en Aardrijkskunde in een andere dan de moedertaal (History and Geography in the first foreign language), Report of Seminar held in Bergen E.S., 19 May 1994 (unpublished).

Footnotes

1. This bears interesting comparison with the criteria applied in the corresponding examinations in the Member States, e.g. 40 per cent per subject in Ireland and 50 per cent in Belgium. (See D. Swan, 'A comparative study of examination success and failure in the EU Member States: The Humpty Dumpty Factor', presented at the Conference of ICSEI (International Congress for School Effectiveness and School Improvement) Melbourne, 1994.)

Chapter 3. THE HISTORY, GOVERNANCE AND MULTINATIONAL ACCOUNTABILITY OF THE EUROPEAN SCHOOLS

References

Beare, H. (1993): 'Different Ways of Viewing School-Site Councils: Whose Paradigm is in Use here?' in H. Beare and W. Lowe Boyd (eds), *Restructuring Schools: An International Perspective on the Movement to Transform the Control and Performance of Schools,* London, The Falmer Press, p.206.

Caldwell, B.J. (1993): 'Paradox and Uncertainty in the Governance of Education' in H. Beare and W. Lowe Boyd (eds), op.cit. p.166.

Commission of the European Communities (1986b): Memorandum on the Motion for a Resolution by Mrs Peus. Presented at the joint public hearing of the European Parliament's Committee on Youth, Culture, Education, Information and Sport, and Committee on Budgetary Control, on the European Schools, 26-27 November, PE 109.260.

European Parliament (1986a): Committee on Budgetary Control, Draft Report on the use of Subsidies from the Community budget to the European Schools, (Rapporteur: K. Schön) 2 October 1986, PE 102.454, p.8, item 13. Op.cit., p.7, item 8.

European Parliament (1986b) Committee on Youth, Culture, Education, Information and Sport, Working Document on the European Schools, Rapporteur Mrs G. Peus, 1 April, PE 103.068, p.1.

European Schools (1984): Enquiry into the Working of the European Schools,

Report of the Primary Board of Inspectors, 2 October, EE/1694/84 EN.
European Schools (1988), Report to the Board of Governors, 23 December, EE/2215/88/EN.
Van Houtte, A. (1984), European Parliament: Committee on Youth, Culture, Education, Information and Sport. Annex 4 to the Report of the Working Party by Dr Peus, 20 April 1984, EE/10581, 84-EN.

Footnote

1. Austria, Finland and Sweden were added as from 1 January 1995.

Chapter 4. THE SCHOOL COMMUNITIES OF TEACHERS, PARENTS AND PUPILS

References

Beattie, Nicholas (1978): 'Formalized Parental Participation in Education: A Comparative Perspective (France, German Federal Republic, England and Wales), *Comparative Education*, 14, March . Cited in H. Beare and W. Lowe Boyd (eds), *Restructuring Schools*, London, The Falmer Press, 1993, p.201.

Blomme, L., C. Maffioli and D. Pickersgill (1989): 'An Assessment of the European School, Bergen by its ex-pupils', *Schola Europaea*, XII, No. 105, 5-28.

Council of the European Union (1994): Convention Defining the Statute of the European Schools, Brussels, 2 June, 7060/94,Conv/EE/en.

European Parliament (1986): 'Report drawn up on behalf of the Committee on Youth, Culture, Education, Information and Sport, on the European Schools ', Rapporteur Mrs G. Peus, Document A2-244186.

European Parliament (1986a): Memorandum from the European Schools' Staff Committee to the European Parliament on the teacher qualifications and mobility. Statement submitted to Public Hearing of Committee on Youth, Culture, Education, Information and Sport, November (mimeo).

Fitzgerald, K. and E. O'Leary (1990): 'Cross-cultural Counselling: Counsellors' Views on Barriers, Benefits, Personal Qualities and Necessary Preparation', *Irish Journal of Psychology*, 11, 3, 238-48.

Headmasters(1984): Statement to the European Parliament on the Draft Report of the Committee on Youth, Culture and Education on the European Schools, November.

Inspectors' Enquiry into the Working of the European Schools, Report of the Primary Board of Inspectors, 2 October 1984, EE/1694/84/EN, p.8.

Kelly, Seán (1970): *Teaching in the City*, Dublin, Gill and Macmillan.

Macbeth, Alastair, *et al.* (1982): *The Child Between, A Report on School-Family Relations in the Countries of the European Community*, Luxembourg and Brussels, Office for Official Publications of the European Communities.

McLean, Martin (1990): *Britain and a Single Market Europe: Prospects for a Common*

School Curriculum, London, Kogan Page, in association with the Institute of Education, University of London.

Mallinson, Vernon (1980): *The European Idea in Education,* Oxford, Pergamon Press.

Opitz, W. (1990): 'Europädagogik die Europäischen Schulen', *Schola Europaea,* XII, No.109, 5-14.

Pritchard, Rosalind M. A., (1981): 'Pupil and Parent Representation in Ireland and Germany', *Comparative Education,* Vol.1, No. 3, 271-84.

Sheridan, Rosaleen (1978): Specific Psychological Problems of the Transient Adolescent, MPsychSc Thesis, University College Dublin, unpublished, p.158.

Swan, D. (1974): A National Survey of Reading Standards and Related Factors in First Year Students in Irish Post Primary Schools, PhD Thesis, University College Dublin, pp.196-97.

Van Houtte, A. (1984): Annex 4 to the Report by the Working Party of the European Parliament, 20.4.1984, E E/1058/84 – EN, p.5.

Wall, W.D. (1977): *Constructive Education for Adolescents,* London, Harrap; Paris, UNESCO.

Footnote

1. As we have seen, because of the introduction of the Intermediate evaluation this situation no longer obtains.

Chapter 5. THE EUROPEAN SCHOOLS – THEIR ACHIEVEMENTS, PROBLEMS AND WIDER SIGNIFICANCE

References

Hart, M. (1992): *The European Dimension in General Primary and Secondary Education,* Alkmaar, The Netherlands: Centre for International Education.

Husén, T., A. Tuijnman and W.D. Halls (eds) (1992): *Schooling in Modern European Society – A Report of the Academia Europaea,* Oxford, Pergamon Press.

McLean, Martin (1990): *Britain and a Single Market Europe: Prospects for a Common School Curriculum,* London, Kogan Page, in association with the Institute of Education, University of London.

Nordenbo, Sven Erik (1993): 'What is implied by a "European Curriculum"? Issues of Eurocentrism, Rationality and Education' in B. Kruithof and S. Sting (eds), *Education and Modernization: The European Experience,* Amsterdam, NESA (Network Educational Science), 12-21.

Shennan, M. (1991) *Teaching about Europe,* London and New York, Cassells.

ADDRESSES

European School of Luxembourg
Boulevard Konrad Adenauer 23
L-1115 Luxembourg/Kirchberg
Luxembourg

European School of Varese/Ispra
Via Montello 118
1-21100 Verese
Italy

European School of Brussels I/Uccle
Avenue du Vert Chasseur 46
B-1180 Brussels
Belgium

European School of Karlsruhe
Albert Schweitzer Straβ 1
D-7500 Karlsruhe 1
Germany

European School of Mol/Geel
Europawijk 100
B-2400 Mol
Belgium

European School of Bergen
 NH/Petten
Molenweidtje 5
1860 AB Bergen NH
The Netherlands

European School of Brussels
 II/Woluwe
Avenue Oscar Jespers 75
B-1200 Brussels
Belgium

European School of Munich
Elise-Aulinger Straβ 21
D-81730 München 83
Germany

European School of Culham
Culham
Abingdon
Oxfordshire OX14 3DZ
UK

INDEX

academic standards, 35
admission to University, 61
Adorno, T.W., 29
A-levels (British), 38, 62
alternativism, 37
Alvanos, Mr, 16
Aristotle, 32
art, 44, 50
assimilation, 12, 20, 33, 120, 123
auslandsschulen ('schools abroad'), 21
Austria, 29, 62, 67

Baetens Beardsmore, H., 64
Beare, H., 80
Belgium, 3, 31, 38, 43 67
 – education system, 81
 – Ministry of Education, 2
Bildung, 37
bilingual education, 7, 65, 123
Biology, 54, 57 (*see also* natural sciences)
Blomme, L., 23, 30, 63
Bogh, 16
Briggs, A., 61
Broadfoot, P., 39
Buchan, J., 16
Bulwer, J.D., 30, 64

Caldwell, B., 82
Chemistry, 57 (*see also* natural sciences)
child development, 39
Clarotti, G., 20, 22
Collège d'Europe, Bruges, 15
Comenius, 32
communicative approach, 45
company schools, 33
complementary activities, 49, 50
Council of Europe, 65
cultural analysis, 37
cultural identity, 47
cultural nationalism, 27
cultures, incommensurateness of, 20
curricula, national, 43

Delors, Jacques, 14
democratic values, 39
Denmark, 29, 34, 38, 40, 67, 88, 123
Department of Education and Science (Department for Education) (UK), 39, 61, 62, 63
disability, pupils with, 48, 118
Doyle, L., 24

Eastern bloc European countries, 123
Economic and Social Sciences, 53, 54
economics, 57, 58
education, European dimension, 28

135

elective subjects, 53, 57
elite, 39
Elliott, Mr, 18, 24
encyclopaedism, 38, 39, 41, 56
England, 9, 40, 56, 62
England and Wales, 38, 56
Environmental studies, 44, 45, 77
epistemology, 39
Erikson, Erik, 27
Eton, 24, 25
ETUC (European Trade Union Confederation), 2
'Eurocentrism', 37
'Euromaths', 48, 77
Europeanism, 126
European Atomic Energy Community (EAEC), 68; Research Centres at Ispra 68, Geel 68, Petten 68, Joint European Thorus, 69
European Baccalaureate, 10, 13, 19, 21, 35, 42, 55, 58-63
- administration, 59, 60
- comparison with A-levels (UK), 121
- creation of, 70
- grade inflation, 59
- success rate, 58
- marking scheme, 59, 60
- oral tests, 59
- recognition of, 61-3, 83, 125
- regulations of, 71
- structure, 59, 60
- subject choice, 84, 104, 116
- success rate, 58
- written tests, 59
European Coal and Steel Community (ECSC), 68, 69, 71
European Commission, 65, 72, 76, 81
European Economic Community (EEC), 68
European Council, 18
European curriculum, 125
European dimension of curriculum, 23, 28, 63, 65, 66, 123

European Education Systems, 7
'European hour', 44, 46, 47, 78
'European ideal', the, 23, 35, 120
European identity, 26, 65, 120, 125
European mentality, 120
European Parliament, 1, 2, 7, 15, 18, 22, 81, 103
- Committee on Youth, Culture, Education Information, Sport and Budgetary Controls, 3, 16, 72, 74, 79
- members of, 13
European Patent Office, 69, 71, 114
European School:
- Bergen, 3, 9, 13, 15, 21, 23, 30, 63, 68, 109, 111
- Brussels I (Uccle), 3, 9, 68, 88, 109, 111
- Brussels II (Woluwe), 3, 9, 17, 68, 88, 109, 111
- Brussels III, 9, 70
- Culham, 3, 9, 21, 63, 65, 69, 77, 91, 109, 111
- Karlsruhe, 9, 68, 109, 111
- Luxembourg, 9, 13, 14, 16, 17, 63, 69, 77, 88, 111
- Mol, 3, 9, 14, 68, 69, 88, 109, 111
- Munich, 9, 69, 108, 111
- Varese, 3, 9, 10, 13, 61, 62, 68, 69, 109, 111, 123
European Schools, the, 6, 7, 8, 32, 33, as reference points for pupils, 107
- nursery school/kindergarten, 8, 46, 68, 78, 111
- primary level, 8, 12
- primary education council, 77
- secondary level, 8, 48, 50, 51, 54, 77, 84
- secondary education council, 77
- observation period, 48, 49-52 *passim*, 70
- orientation period, 48, 56-8

Index

- accountability, 80, 81
- administration, quality of, 81, 83
- administrative and financial committee (CAF), 73, 74
- administrative boards, 73, 76, 80
- admissions policy, 8, 32, 110
- authority structure, 80, 84
- Board of Governors (Conseil Supérieur), 9, 17, 22, 24, 41-3, 47, 49, 59, 68, 70-73, 76, 78, 80-83, 89, 117
- centralisation, 82, 84
- Conseillers d'Education, 91
- costliness of, 24, 25, 35
- curriculum, 7, 25, 36-66 *passim*
  reform, 98
- dates of establishment, 69
- deputy directors, 76, 77
- deputy Secretary-General, 74
- disabled pupils, 84
- Enlarged Teaching Committee, 73, 75, 78
- enrolment, 10, 22, 104, 108-11
  fluctuations in, 108-11
  policy, 113-15
- 'entitled pupils', 33, 105, 109-11
- equality of esteem, 10, 20, 123
- extra-curricular activities, 73
- funding, 18, 67, 70, 71
- governance, 67, 72, 83
- grade repetition, 83
- heads of department, 121
- history of, 67-70 *passim*
- inclusiveness of, 29, 84
- innovations in, 85
- Intermediate evaluation, the, 55, 83, 85
- internal management and consultation, 79
- inspectors, 2, 8, 61, 72, 75, 80, 89
- isolation, 12, 19, 84, 120
- language in the curriculum, 7, 11, 12
- language sections, 11, 122
- language teaching, 98
- *langues véhiculaires*, 12, 44, 50, 51, 54, 57, 58, 64, 65, 70, 85, 95
- legal status, 10, 68, 69, 70
- maintenance, 72
- 'non-entitled pupils', 111
- organisational structures, 72-81 *passim*
- overcrowding, 109
- parents, 2, 4, 68, 70, 80, 87, 99-104 *passim*, 112
  concerns of, 99
  contribution of, to the Schools, 102, 103
  need of, for information, 99
  representatives of, 76-8, 103
- parent-teacher meetings, 103
- Parents' Association (Interparents), 72, 73, 78
- pupils, 19, 87, 104-18 *passim*, 122
  achievements of, 116
  attitudes of, 104
  attitudes of, to school, 115, 116
  counselling of, 98, 108
  dropout of, from Schools, 117
  emotional problems of, 106-8
  expatriate status of, 105-7
  failure rates of, 17, 35, 84, 105
  guidance of, 53, 84, 105
  home conditions of, 106
  individual differences of, 104-5
  leisure time of, 106
  national origins of, 104
  enrolment rate of, 112
  pastoral care of, 53, 98
  problems of, 116
  promotion of, 78, 83
  representatives of, 76, 78
- responsiveness of system, 85
- school annuals, 90
- school buildings, 72, 104
- school directors (Heads), 74-7, 82, 92, 103, 117

137

A Singular Pluralism

- school size, 93, 104, 108, 109
- school tours, 89, 102
- school transport, 73, 102
- Secretary-General (Representative of the Board of Governors), 72-6
- secretariate, 74
- significance of, 119
- statute, 13, 26, 52, 61, 70
- statute (1994), 71, 82
- staff committee, 72, 73
- staff meetings, 78
- subject coordinators, 79, 85, 97, 98
- syllabus, 37, 40, 70, 71
- teachers, 8, 25, 70, 76, 85, 87, 88-91 *passim*
  - and adaptation problems, 104
  - and language teaching, 95
  - and parents, 99
  - and task, 93-7 *passim*
  - appointment of, 90, 91
  - as surrogate parents, 108
  - attitudes of, 94
  - *chargé de cours*, 91
  - initial training of, 97, 120
  - inservice training of, 72, 84, 97
  - national origins of, 89
  - national styles of teaching, 40, 97, 103, 104
  - role of, 94
  - secondments, 90, 97
  - selection of, 91, 92, 97
  - and stress, 95
- textbooks, 25, 120
- working parties, 73

European Union (EU), 1, 6, 7, 8, 10, 19, 51
- Commission of the, 7, 15, 17, 19, 65, 72, 76
- Directorate General XXII (Task Force on Human Resources, Education, Training, Youth and Sport), 14, 15
- Ministers for Education, 10, 18, 30, 71, 72
- Departments of Education, 68
- Directive on teaching mobility (1992), 98
- Educational dimension of, 126
- Member States of, 6, 7, 11, 13, 15, 20, 55, 68, 69, 71, 80

European Unification, 126
European University Institute, Florence, 15
'Euro-rhetoric', 27
'Eurosceptics', 27
Eurydice, Irish office of, 2
examinations, 56
- school leaving, 59

family relocation, 47
failure, academic, 33, 53
Federation de la Function Publique Européene (FFPE), 23, 128
Finland, 29, 63
Foulkes, J., 62
fourth language, 53, 54, 57
France, 3, 38, 39, 40, 52, 58, 67, 123
- education system (Loi Haby), 81, 101
- Ministry of Education, 2, 3, 13

Geography, 45, 49, 51, 53, 54, 57 (*see also* Human Sciences), 58, 59
Germany, 38, 40, 58, 62, 67
- teachers' and pupils' attitudes to each other, 101
- Ministry of Education, 2
Germany, West, 3
Graphic Arts, 49, 50
Greece, 29, 34, 38, 58, 67, 88
- Ministry of Education, 2
Greek, Ancient, 53, 54, 57
guidance and pastoral care of pupils, 53, 120

138

Halls, W.D., 14, 28, 63, 119
handwriting, 46
Hart, Michael, 14, 40, 59, 65
History, 45, 49, 51, 53, 54, 57 (*see also* Human Sciences), 58, 59, 64, 65
holidays, 40
humanism, 38, 41, 56
Human Sciences (*see* History and Geography)
Husén, T., 119

identity, European, 27, 28, 29, 30
identity formation, 27
identity, national, 26, 28, 29, 30
IMCO (Staff Committee of the European Council), 2
Integrated Science (Biology, Physics and Chemistry), 50, 52
Intermediate Examinations (Belgium, France, Germany, Ireland, Italy, Luxembourg, Netherlands, UK), 55
International baccalaureate, 59
International baccalaureate Schools, 66
International Bureau of Education, 40
Ireland, 34, 38, 43, 67, 82, 88, 101
– Department of Education, 2
Italy, 10, 38, 40, 58, 67, 101

Kellett-Bowman, E., 16
Kohls, J., 64

Latin, 49, 50, 54, 57
Lewis, A., 23, 128
lifelong learning, 122
local history, 52
Luxembourg, 10, 11, 38, 43, 67, 88, 89
– Ministry of Education, 2
lycée, 58

Maastricht Treaty, 19, 34, 81, 125
Macbeth, A., 100, 101

Mallinson, Vernon, 14, 67
Mann, Thomas, 38
Mapes, G., 26
Marshall, J., 24
Mathematics, 44, 49, 50, 52, 54, 57, 59
McLean, M., 38, 41, 42, 124
migrants, education of, 14
Mikes, G., 36
minority cultures, 126
Mitbestimmungsgesetz ('co-determination law'), 80, 101
Model European Council and Parliament, 65
Monnet, Jean, 13, 14, 27
Morin, E., 36
mother tongue (L1), 43, 44, 45, 49, 50, 51, 54, 57, 111
Murphy, I., 26
Music, 44, 49, 50, 54, 57

Namur Conference Report, 21, 25, 66
national idioms of education, 41, 42
national myths and stereotypes, 35
national perspectives on education, 29, 30, 38, 39, 40
national school systems, 126
National University of Ireland, 61, 62
nationalism in education, 28, 29, 35, 126
nationality, European, 30
naturalist, 38, 39, 41
Natural Sciences (Physics, Chemistry and Biology), 49, 53, 55, 59
Neave, G., 14
neo-Nazism, 29
Netherlands/Holland, 2, 30, 38, 40, 67, 123
New Zealand, 82
Noord Holland Dagblad, 26
Nordenbo, S.E., 37, 39, 124
Northern Ireland, 38, 56
nursery education, 43

O'Brien, B., 17
Olsen, J., 1, 74
Ó Néill, P., 46, 130
Oostlander, A.M., 18, 20, 34
Opitz, W., 38, 45

Papapietro, Mr, 16
parental involvement with schools, 39, 100-2
pedagogia, 37
pedagogy, 32, 40
pedagogy, European, 33
pedagogies, national, 33, 53
Pedini, Mr, 16
Pery, Mrs, 16
Peus Report, 81, 92, 110, 113, 114
Philosophy, 57-9, 63, 70
Physical Education, 44, 49, 50, 54, 57
Physics, 57 (*see also* Natural Sciences)
Piaget, 32
Pinck, G., 74
Plastic Arts, 50, 54, 57
pluralism, 6, 12, 34, 120, 126
Portugal, 29, 34, 38, 58, 67, 88
– Ministry of Education, 2
post-nationalist Europe, 7
Pritchard, R. (1981), 101
Pruvot, Ms, 16
Psychology, 58

Quintilian, 32

reconstructionism, 27
reconstructionist, 37
recreation, 44
'Reform Committee', 42, 43, 47
religion/ethics, 44, 46, 49, 50, 52, 57
remedial teachers, 98
remedial teaching, 47, 48, 51, 84, 104, 118, 120
Rome, Treaty of, 14, 34
Ryan, M., 24

Scandinavian countries, 123
Schlesinger, P., 27
Schola Europaea, 3, 87, 89, 103
school boards, 80
school psychologists, 72
Scotland, 38, 56
– Ministry of Education, 2
Scuola Normale Superiore, 62
Shennan, M., 126
Sheridan, R., 107
Sicily, 63
Single European Act (1987), 125
Sociology, 57, 58
Spain, 29, 34, 38, 58, 67, 88
– Ministry of Education, 2
Spaak, Paul-Henri, 6
subjects, compulsory, 56, 57, 58
Swan, T.D., 17, 20, 106
Sweden, 29
Switzerland, 62

The Independent, 24
The Times Educational Supplement, 24
third language (L3), 50, 54, 57
Thygesen, J.C., 16
timetables, 40
tolerance, 98, 120
Tosi, A., 20, 64, 129
Tuijnman, A., 119

United Kingdom, 29, 34, 38, 67, 82
United Nation's School, New York, 22
United States of America, 15, 28, 82

Van der Spek, C., 45, 51
Van Houtte, A., 17, 70, 114

Walkhoff Report, 81
Wall, W.D., 106, 133
Wall Street Journal, The, 26
Wathelet, F., 23, 129
Webster, Noah, 28
Woolf, M., 21, 24
World Wars, 29